Bridging 1 to 2

Summer SPLASH

LEARNING ACTIVITIES

Brighter Child®
An imprint of Carson-Dellosa Publishing LLC
Greensboro, North Carolina

Brighter Child®
An imprint of Carson-Dellosa Publishing LLC
P.O. Box 35665
Greensboro, NC 27425 USA

Printed in the USA • All rights reserved.   ISBN 978-1-60996-968-4

02-081121151

Table of Contents

Making the Most of
Summer Splash Learning Activities

This resource contains a myriad of fun and challenging reading and math activities. The reading pages provide practice in long and short vowels, sequencing, classification, and reading for details. The math pages review skills taught in first grade, such as basic addition and subtraction, time and money, and measurement.

Most of the activities in the book are designed so that your child can work independently. However, your child will enjoy the activities much more if you work alongside him or her. Make sure to let your child know that this is not a workbook with tests, but a book of fun activities that you can do together. The book is divided into 10 weeks, with eight activity pages per week. Feel free to choose how many per day and in which order you do the activities, but complete the weeks in sequence, since activities become increasingly challenging as the book progresses.

Summer Splash Learning Activities provides an important link between your child's first- and second-grade school years. It reviews what your child learned in first grade, providing the confidence and skills that he or she needs for the coming fall. The activities in this book will help your child successfully bridge the gap between first and second grade by reviewing and reinforcing the important and essential skills for his or her continued academic success. These activities are designed to

- review skills in math, reading, and language arts that your child learned the previous year.

- give you an opportunity to monitor your child's skills in various areas.

- offer you a chance to spend special time with your child.

- enable your child to continue routine daily learning activities.

- give you a chance to praise your child's efforts.

- demonstrate to your child that you value lifetime learning.

- make you an active and important part of your child's educational development.

Getting Started

In order for your child to get the most from the activities in this resource, use these helpful tips to make these learning experiences interesting and, most of all, fun!

- Set aside a time each day for completing the activities. Make it a time when your child will be most ready to learn, and make it a routine.
- Provide a pleasant, quiet place to work. This means no TV in your child's work area. Also, make sure there is a sufficient light source.
- Review in advance the activity page(s) your child will complete that session. This way, you will be able to familiarize yourself with the lesson.
- Have your child read the directions aloud beforehand to make sure he or she understands the activity. Instructions are written for the child, but he or she may need your help reading and/or understanding them.
- Let your child help choose which activity he or she would like to complete that day.
- Praise all your child's work. It's the effort, not necessarily the end result, that counts most.

No one knows better than you how your child learns best, so use this book to enhance the way you already work with him or her. Use every opportunity possible as a learning experience, whether making a trip through the grocery store or riding in the car. Pose problems and let your child figure out how to solve them, asking questions such as *Which route should we take to the park? What could we use to make a plant grow straight?* or *How high should we hang this shelf?* Also, respond excitedly to discoveries your child makes throughout the day with comments such as *That rock is really unique! I wonder how long it took the spider to spin that web;* or *You spent your money wisely.* In this way, you will encourage and motivate your child to learn throughout the day and for the rest of his or her life, providing the confidence and self-esteem he or she needs for continued academic success.

Everyday Learning Activities

Use these simple educational activities to keep your child's mind engaged and active during the summer months and all year long!

- Ask your child to make a schedule of events for the day, in the order in which they will take place. Ask him or her to prioritize the list and number the events.

- On a neighborhood walk or while driving in the car, encourage your child to read all the street signs and numbers.

- Read with your child each day. Encourage your child to retell the story to you. Then, have him or her make up original adventures for the story characters or write an additional chapter.

- Have your child write down important dates such as family birthdays, important trips or outings, or holidays. Be sure your child capitalizes the name of the month and week and uses a comma between the day and year.

- During a visit to the park or playground, invite your child to describe what he or she sees there, using as many adjectives as possible.

- Have your child list three things you can smell, feel, taste, or see in a particular room of the house or on a "senses walk."

- Have your child identify as many parts of the human body as he or she can. Ask him or her to describe the function of each part, if possible.

- Ask your child to read a recipe with you for a simple dish. Practice measuring skills by simulating measuring out the ingredients with water or rice in measuring spoons or cups.

- Have your child read the price of items in a store or supermarket. Challenge him or her to estimate how much can be bought with a designated amount of money. Can your child figure out how much change is left over?

- Encourage your child to tell you whether certain objects in your home (sofa, pencil) would be measured in pounds or ounces.

- Fill a measuring cup with water to different levels, and invite your child to read the measurement and then write it as a fraction.

- Encourage your child to read nonfiction library books and make up creative stories about the subject matter (e.g., lions or airplanes).

Assessment

Circle the letter that will complete each word in 1–5.

1. cl _o_ ck   a e i (o) u

2. t ī re   a e (i) o u

3. h _a_ nd   (a) e i o u

4. b _e_ e   a (e) i o u

5. tr _u_ ck   a e i o (u)

Use the information below to answer questions 6–9. Circle your choice.

Trees can be divided into two groups: evergreen and deciduous. Evergreen trees keep their leaves throughout the year. Their leaves are often shaped like needles. Christmas trees are evergreens.

Deciduous trees lose their leaves in the fall. They grow new leaves in the spring. Deciduous trees may also grow flowers or fruit. Trees that turn red, orange, or yellow in the fall are deciduous.

6. Which of these would be a good title for the passage?
   A. Christmas Trees
   B. Trees with Needles
   C. The Changing Leaves
   D. Two Types of Trees

Assessment

7. Deciduous trees are more beautiful than evergreen trees.
   A. fact
   B. opinion

8. _C._____ trees are evergreens.
   A. Needles   **B.** Orange
   C. Christmas   **D.** Deciduous

9. This information is _Fact_.
   A. fact
   B. fantasy

Circle the word that does not belong.

10. red   blue   orange   ~~banana~~

11. moon   (bike)   sun   stars

Read the story to answer questions 12–17.

Tommy was tired of the way that Aaron and his friends treated him at school. They always took the ball away from him during recess and broke his pencils at the writing center. His mom told him to forget about it. Tommy could not. He had a better idea.

Tommy brought a package to school with Aaron's name on it. Aaron was confused. "What is this?" he asked.

"Open it," Tommy replied.

Inside, Aaron found a ball and a package of pencils. "Now you will have your own," Tommy said. Aaron smiled.

12. How would you describe Aaron at the beginning of the story?
   A. mean   **B.** nice
   C. friendly   **D.** funny

Assessment

13. How are Aaron and Tommy alike?

    A. They are not friendly.   **B.** They go to the same school.

    C. They like to break pencils.   **D.** They solve problems wisely.

14. What was the effect of Tommy bringing a package to school with Aaron's name on it?

    A. Aaron broke his pencils.

    B. Tommy's mom told him to forget about it.

    C. Aaron was confused.

    D. Tommy had a better idea.

15. Put the following sentences in the correct order to tell what happened in the story.

    4 Aaron smiled at Tommy.

    1 Aaron took Tommy's ball.

    2 Tommy had an idea.

    3 Tommy brought a package to school for Aaron.

16. Write how you think Tommy felt at the beginning of the story.

    Sad

17. Predict what you think happened after Aaron received the package.

    he stoped

18. Follow the directions below.

    1. First, draw three flowers side by side.

    2. Then, color the flower in the middle yellow.

    3. Last, draw a bee on the right flower.

Assessment Analysis

Answer Key:

1.	o	7.	B.	13.	B.
2.	i	8.	C.	14.	C.
3.	a	9.	A.	15.	4, 1, 2, 3
4.	e	10.	banana	16.	Answers will vary.
5.	u	11.	bike	17.	Answers will vary.
6.	D.	12.	A.	18.	Directions should be followed.

After reviewing the assessment, match the problems answered incorrectly to the corresponding activity pages. Your child should spend extra time on those skills to strengthen his or her reading skills.

Number	Skill	Activity Page(s)
1., 3., 5.	short vowels	14–17
2., 4.	long vowels	22–25
6.	main idea	30–33
7.	fact or opinion	38–39
8.	reading for details	40–41
9.	reality versus fantasy	46–47
10., 11.	classification	48–49
12., 16.	character analysis	54–55
13.	compare and contrast	62–64
14.	cause and effect	70–73
15.	sequencing	56–57, 65
17.	predicting outcomes	78–81
18.	following directions	86–89

Assessm...

Write each numeral.

1. eight _6_   twelve _12_   thirty-seven _37_

Count by twos.

2. 6, _8_ , _10_ , 12, 14, _16_ , _18_ , 20

Count by fives.

3. 0, _5_ , 10, 15, _20_ , _25_ , 30, _35_ , 40

Count by tens.

4. 30, _40_ , _50_ , 60, _70_ , _80_ , 90, _100_

Circle the odd numbers.

5. (1) 2 (3) 4 (5) 6 (7) 8 (9) 10   **6.** 14 (81) (17) 10 34 66 (89)

Write the number of tens and ones.

7. 36 is the same as _3_ tens and _6_ ones.

8. 61 is the same as _6_ tens and _1_ ones.

Solve each problem.

9.

$$6 + 1 = 7$$ $$7 + 6 = 13$$ $$3 + 4 = 7$$ $$6 + 0 = 6$$ $$8 + 1 = 9$$

10.

$$12 - 8 = 4$$ $$9 - 3 = 6$$ $$6 - 4 = 2$$ $$6 - 5 = 1$$ $$7 - 4 = 3$$

11.

$$28 + 13 = 41$$ $$14 + 29 = 43$$ $$86 + 5 = 91$$ $$67 + 17 = 84$$ $$33 + 48 = 81$$

12.

$$84 - 17 = 67$$ $$34 - 19 = 15$$ $$43 - 28$$ $$66 - 48$$ $$52 - 35$$

Assessment

Write the times shown on each clock.

13. 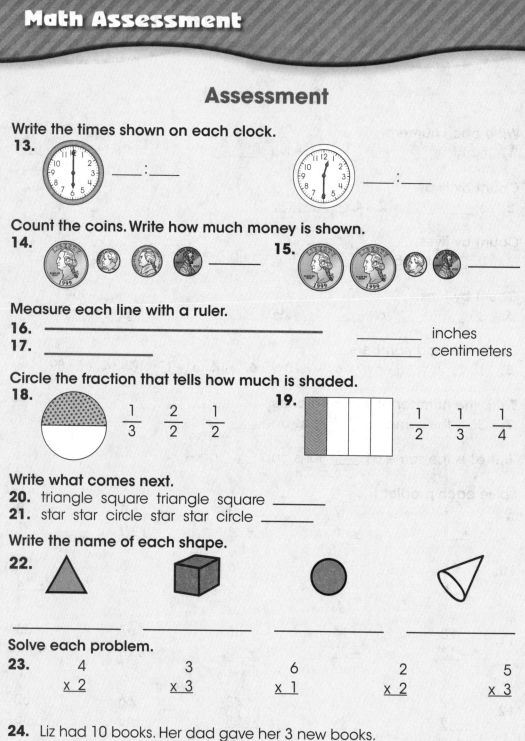 ____ : ____

____ : ____

Count the coins. Write how much money is shown.

14. ____

15. ____

Measure each line with a ruler.

16. ——————————————————————— ____ inches

17. ———————————— ____ centimeters

Circle the fraction that tells how much is shaded.

18. $\frac{1}{3}$ $\frac{2}{2}$ $\frac{1}{2}$

19. $\frac{1}{2}$ $\frac{1}{3}$ $\frac{1}{4}$

Write what comes next.

20. triangle square triangle square _____

21. star star circle star star circle _____

Write the name of each shape.

22.

_____   _____   _____   _____

Solve each problem.

23.
$$\begin{array}{r} 4 \\ \times\,2 \\ \hline \end{array} \qquad \begin{array}{r} 3 \\ \times\,3 \\ \hline \end{array} \qquad \begin{array}{r} 6 \\ \times\,1 \\ \hline \end{array} \qquad \begin{array}{r} 2 \\ \times\,2 \\ \hline \end{array} \qquad \begin{array}{r} 5 \\ \times\,3 \\ \hline \end{array}$$

24. Liz had 10 books. Her dad gave her 3 new books. How many books does Liz have now? _____ books

Assessment Analysis

Answer Key:
1. 8, 12, 37
2. 8, 10, 16, 18
3. 5, 20, 25, 35
4. 40, 50, 70, 80, 100
5. 1, 3, 5, 7, 9
6. 81, 17, 89
7. 3, 6
8. 6, 1

9. 7, 13, 7, 6, 9
10. 4, 6, 2, 1, 3
11. 41, 43, 91, 84, 81
12. 67, 15, 15, 18, 17
13. 6:00, 12:30
14. 41¢ or $0.41
15. 61¢ or $0.61
16. 3 inches
17. 3 centimeters

18. $\frac{1}{2}$
19. $\frac{1}{4}$
20. triangle
21. star
22. triangle, cube, circle, cone
23. 8, 9, 6, 4, 15
24. 13 books

After reviewing the assessment, match the problems answered incorrectly to the corresponding activity pages. Your child should spend extra time on those activities to strengthen his or her math skills.

Number	Skill	Activity Page(s)
1., 2., 3., 4., 5., 6., 7., 8.	numeration	18–21, 26–29
9.	basic addition	34–37
10.	basic subtraction	42–45
11.	advanced addition	50–53
12.	advanced subtraction	58–61
13., 14., 15.	time and money	66–69, 74–75
16., 17.	measurement	76–77
18., 19.	fractions	82–83
20., 21., 22.	patterns and geometry	84–85
23.	multiplication	90–91
24.	problem solving	92–93

Germs

Read the passage below.

Germs are things you should not share. Germs can make you sick. Even though you cannot see germs, they get into the body in many ways. Germs get in the body through the nose, mouth, eyes, and cuts in the skin. We share germs when we sneeze or cough and do not cover our mouths. We share germs when we drink from the same cup or eat from the same plate.

To keep germs to yourself and to get well:

- Wash your hands with soap.
- Cover your mouth when you cough or sneeze.
- Do not share food or drink.
- Keep your fingers away from your nose, mouth, and eyes.
- Drink lots of water.
- Get lots of fresh air.
- Eat healthy meals.
- Get plenty of sleep.

Germs

Answer the following questions using the passage on page 14.

1. What is the main idea?

   A. Germs are things you do not want to share.

   B. You can't see germs.

   C. Wash your hands often.

2. Put an *X* next to the ways you can keep germs to yourself.

   ____Wash your hands with soap.

   ____Stay away from animals.

   ____Cover your mouth when you cough or sneeze.

   ____Get plenty of sleep.

   ____Eat healthy meals.

3. Put a *T* next to the sentences that are true. Put an *F* next to the sentences that are false.

   ____Germs can make you sick.

   ____Germs cannot get in your body through the nose, mouth, eyes, and cuts in the skin.

   ____Cover your mouth when you cough or sneeze to keep germs to yourself.

Choose the correct short vowel.

4. Germs can make you s ___ ck.

   i   o

5. Germs get in the body through c ___ ts in the skin.

   a   u

6. Cover your mo ___ th when you cough.

   o   u

7. Get l ___ ts of fresh air.

   i   o

Use the dictionary entry below to answer the questions.

> **germ** (jûrm), n. 1. a disease-producing microbe. 2. a bud or seed.

8. What part of speech is *germ*?

   _____

9. Use the word *germ* in a sentence.

   _____

   _____

   _____

Abby

Read the story below.

My dog, Abby, loves to go to the river. Every Saturday morning, I take Abby to the park by the river to play. The first thing Abby does when we get there is run down to the water.

Abby likes to splash in the water. The cold water doesn't bother her. When she gets out of the water, she shakes and shakes. I stand back so that the water does not get on me. Then, she looks for a rock in the sun to take a nap on. She sleeps there until I whistle for her when it is time to go home.

I think our Saturday trips to the river are something that Abby looks forward to all week.

Abby

Answer the following questions using the story on page 16.

1. What is the main idea?
   - **A.** Abby takes a nap.
   - **B.** Abby loves trips to the river.
   - **C.** Abby is a good dog.

2. Number the events in the order that they happened in the story.
   ___ I whistle for Abby when it is time to go home.
   ___ Abby runs to the water.
   ___ Abby takes a nap.
   ___ Abby splashes in the water.

3. What does Abby do when she gets out of the water?
   - **A.** rolls in the dirt
   - **B.** shakes and shakes
   - **C.** licks her fur

Choose the correct short vowel.

4. I have a d ___ g.
   i   o

5. Abby likes to spl ___ sh in the water.
   a   i

6. Abby n ___ ps on a rock.
   i   a

7. Abby finds a rock in the s ___ n.
   u   a

Sometimes the same word can be used as a noun or as a verb. Write *noun* or *verb* to tell how the bold word is used in each sentence.

8. Can I have a **drink,** please?
   _____

9. My dogs **drink** a lot of water.
   _____

10. My dog made a big **splash** in the water.
    _____

11. The children **splash** in the water.
    _____

12. I order a **shake** with my burger.
    _____

13. My hands **shake** when I am nervous.
    _____

Applying Number Words

0–zero	1–one	2–two	3–three	4–four
5–five	6–six	7–seven	8–eight	9–nine
10–ten	11–eleven	12–twelve		

Use the number words above to help you answer each question.

1. Three comes after _____ .

2. Seven is one less than _____ .

3. Two comes between _____ and _____ .

4. Twelve is one more than _____ .

5. Zero comes before _____ .

6. Eight comes between _____ and _____ .

7. Three comes between _____ and _____ .

8. Nine comes after _____ .

9. Five is two more than _____ .

10. Ten comes before _____ .

11. One is one less than _____ .

12. Four is one more than _____ .

13. Six comes between _____ and _____ .

14. Eleven is two more than _____ .

15. Seven is one more than _____ .

Three-Digit Number Names

The names for numbers with three or more digits do not include the word **and**. For example, the number 323 is written **three hundred twenty-three.** It is not correct to write *three hundred and twenty-three.*

Find the written name for each numeral. Then, use the code to answer the riddle.

Why didn't Benjamin Franklin speak when he experimented with electricity?

110	798		476	856	998		101	206

	998		110		202		467		685	!

eight hundred fifty-six	**A**	seven hundred ninety-eight	**E**
one hundred one	**I**	four hundred sixty-seven	**C**
one hundred ten	**H**	nine hundred ninety-eight	**S**
four hundred seventy-six	**W**	two hundred six	**N**
two hundred two	**O**	six hundred eighty-five	**K**

Counting by Twos and Threes

> To count by 2, color every second number to make a pattern. To count by 3, color every third number to make a different pattern.

1. **Count by twos. Color each numeral that you count.**
   What pattern do you see?

1	2	3	4	5	6	7	8	9	10
11	12	13	14	15	16	17	18	19	20
21	22	23	24	25	26	27	28	29	30
31	32	33	34	35	36	37	38	39	40

2. **Count by threes. Color each numeral that you count.**
   How is this pattern different than the one above?

1	2	3	4	5	6	7	8	9	10
11	12	13	14	15	16	17	18	19	20
21	22	23	24	25	26	27	28	29	30
31	32	33	34	35	36	37	38	39	40

Fill in each missing numeral. Count by twos or threes.

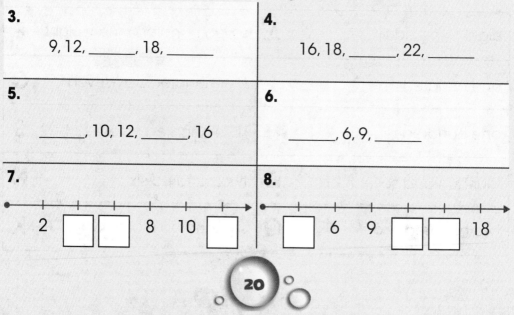

3.
   9, 12, _____, 18, _____

4.
   16, 18, _____, 22, _____

5.
   _____, 10, 12, _____, 16

6.
   _____, 6, 9, _____

7.
   2 ☐ ☐ 8 10 ☐

8.
   ☐ 6 9 ☐ ☐ 18

Counting by Fives and Tens

> To count by 5, color every fifth number to make a pattern. To count by 10, color every tenth number to make a different pattern.

1. Count by fives. Color each numeral that you count with a yellow crayon. Then, count by tens. Color each numeral that you count with a red crayon. What do you notice?

1	2	3	4	5	6	7	8	9	10
11	12	13	14	15	16	17	18	19	20
21	22	23	24	25	26	27	28	29	30
31	32	33	34	35	36	37	38	39	40
41	42	43	44	45	46	47	48	49	50
51	52	53	54	55	56	57	58	59	60
61	62	63	64	65	66	67	68	69	70
71	72	73	74	75	76	77	78	79	80
81	82	83	84	85	86	87	88	89	90
91	92	93	94	95	96	97	98	99	100

Fill in each missing numeral. Count by fives and tens.

2.

    5, _____, _____, 20, 25

3.

    _____, _____, 70, 80, 90, _____

4.

    75, _____, _____, _____, 95

5.

    10, _____, _____, _____, _____, 60

6.

    30, _____, _____, 45, 50, _____, _____, _____

Teddy

Read the poem below.

Mom and Dad think I'm too old
to still have my teddy bear.
They say, "You are eight years old now,
and Teddy shows too much wear."
I nod my head and then agree.
I know I'm a real strong kid.
Without a thought I put him up,
and in my closet he hid.

That same night, I tried and tried,
but could not fall asleep.
A storm came in with lots of noise.
I did not make a peep.
Instead, I took my bear out
of the hiding place I made.
I did not need him to fall asleep.
I just knew he was afraid.

Teddy

Answer the following questions using the poem on page 22.

1. Why do the parents want the child to put the teddy bear away?

   A. They think that the child is too old to have a teddy bear.

   B. They think that the child will lose the bear.

   C. They want the child to play with other toys.

   D. They think that teddy bears are silly.

2. Why couldn't the child in the poem fall asleep?

   A. The child was cold.

   B. The child was worried that the parents were angry.

   C. The child was hungry.

   D. The child thought that the teddy bear was afraid.

3. What did the child do when there was a storm?

   A. went into Mom and Dad's room

   B. got the teddy bear

   C. cried

   D. hid under the covers

4. *Kid* and *hid* are words that rhyme in the poem. Which two words in the pairs below do not rhyme?

   A. *fun* and *run*   B. *bike* and *ride*

   C. *bear* and *tear*   D. *hide* and *side*

5. *Asleep* and *peep* are words in the poem that make the long *e* sound. Which word below does not have the long *e* sound?

   A. read   B. see

   C. agree   D. bed

Twins

Read the story below.

Greg and Tim are twins. They are brothers who were born on the same day. Twins that look almost exactly alike are called identical twins. Greg and Tim do look alike, but they are not identical twins. Greg and Tim are fraternal twins. That means they were born on the same day but do not look exactly alike.

Tim has curly red hair. Greg's hair is brown and straight. Greg has green eyes. Tim's eyes are blue. Another difference between them is their teeth. Greg is missing his two front teeth. Tim has all of his teeth, and he has braces!

Both boys like to play baseball. Sometimes, they play third base. Sometimes, they play catcher. Both of them can throw the ball well. It can be fun to have a twin.

Twins

er the following questions using the story on page 24.
d each phrase. If it describes Greg, write a *G* on the line. If it
cribes Tim, write a *T* on the line. If the phrase describes both
ys, write a *B* on the line.

1. is a twin_____

2. has red hair _____

3. plays catcher _____

4. missing two front teeth_____

5. has green eyes_____

6. Draw a picture of each boy.

7. What do you call twins that do not look exactly alike?

_____

8. Circle the words below that have a long vowel sound.

twin	red	base
teeth	play	fun
braces	Tim	bo

4

5

6.

7.

8.

Ordinal Numbers

When objects are in a particular order, they can be ... ordinal numbers like first, second, third, etc.

Complete each sentence using the words in the Sun.

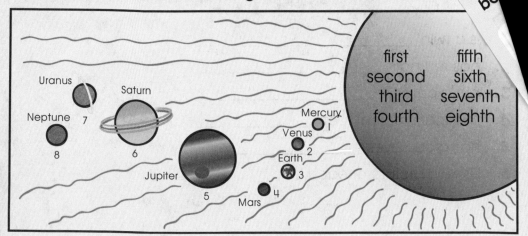

first   fifth
second   sixth
third   seventh
fourth   eighth

1. Mars is the _____ planet from the Sun.

2. Jupiter is the _____ planet from the Sun.

3. Venus is the _____ planet from the Sun.

4. Mercury is the _____ planet from the Sun.

Saturn is the _____ planet from the Sun.

Earth is the _____ planet from the Sun.

Uranus is the _____ planet from the Sun.

Neptune is the _____ planet from the Sun.

Even, Odd, and Ordinal Numbers

Even numbers end in 0, 2, 4, 6, or 8. **Odd numbers** end in 1, 3, 5, 7, or 9.

1. Color the bubbles with odd numbers red. Color the bubbles with even numbers yellow.

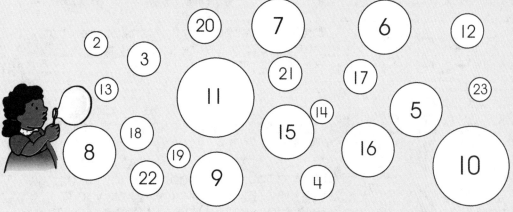

Answer the questions. Start counting from the left.

Grayson   Allie   Denise   Tanner   Lori   Matt   Rob

2. Who is third in line? _____ .

3. Who is sixth in line? _____ .

4. Who is seventh in line? _____ .

5. Who is second in line? _____ .

6. Who is fourth in line? _____ .

27

Place Value: Hundreds, Tens, and Ones

Example: 8 3 4

Circle the number in the ones place. Draw a square around the number in the tens place.

Study the example above. Then, follow the directions below.

1.

5 2 7

Circle the number in the tens place. Draw a triangle around the number in the hundreds place.

2.

9 0 9

Circle the number in the ones place. Draw a square around the number in the hundreds place.

3.

2 4 1

Draw a square around the number in the tens place. Circle the number in the hundreds place. Draw a triangle around the number in the ones place.

4.

1 5 6

Circle the number in the tens place. Draw a triangle around the number in the ones place.

5.

3 1 7

Draw a square around the number in the hundreds place. Cross out the number in the tens place. Circle the number in the ones place.

6.

6 6 2

Draw a triangle around the number in the ones place. Cross out the number in the tens place. Draw a square around the number in the hundreds place.

7.

4 8 5

Circle the number in the hundreds place. Draw a square around the number in the ones place.

Place Value Practice

Study the examples on page 28. Then, write how many hundreds, tens, and ones are in each number.

1. 129 _____ hundreds _____ tens _____ ones

2. 936 _____ hundreds _____ tens _____ ones

3. 462 _____ hundreds _____ tens _____ ones

4. 248 _____ hundreds _____ tens _____ ones

5. 320 _____ hundreds _____ tens _____ ones

6. 863 _____ hundreds _____ tens _____ ones

Write each number.

7. 2 hundreds, 6 tens, 4 ones = _____

8. 7 hundreds, 8 tens, 2 ones = _____

9. 9 hundreds, 1 ten, 4 ones = _____

10. 1 hundred, 5 tens, 3 ones = _____

11. 3 hundreds, 0 tens, 5 ones = _____

12. 3 hundreds, 7 tens, 6 ones = _____

Pandas at the Zoo

> The **main idea** of a story tells what the story is about. It does not tell one part of the story or recall one fact from the story. It is an overview of the entire story or paragraph. Titles often tell you something about the main idea.

The titles below describe the main ideas for the stories on page 31. Look closely at the titles. Write each title at the top of its matching story. Remember to ask yourself, "Does this title tell about the whole story?"

When Yang Yang Is Sick	The Panda Keeper
Becoming a Zookeeper	What Yang Yang Eats

Pandas at the Zoo

See directions on page 30.

1.	2.
Brenda Morgan is a zookeeper in Washington, D.C. Brenda has the very important job of caring for a panda named Yang Yang at the zoo. She is in charge of making sure Yang Yang is happy and healthy.	Brenda always wanted to work closely with animals and help care for them. As a child, Brenda wanted to be a horse when she grew up! Since she could not become a horse, she became a zookeeper instead. Brenda loves her job at the zoo.
3.	**4.**
Part of Brenda's job is to watch Yang Yang closely to be sure he is feeling well. Once, he had an eye infection, and Yang Yang went blind for a few days. Brenda called the veterinarian for medicine, and now Yang Yang is well again.	Yang Yang eats many kinds of foods. He likes gruel, which is made of rice, honey, and cheese. He also enjoys apples and bamboo. Brenda thinks his favorite food is carrots.

Insects

Read each paragraph. Read the sentences. Then, circle the main idea of each paragraph.

1. All insects have six legs. Butterflies and bees have six legs. They are insects. Spiders have eight legs. They are not insects.

   A. Spiders are not insects.

   B. Bees are insects.

   C. Insects have six legs.

2. Insects eat different things. Some insects eat plants. Caterpillars eat leaves. Bees and butterflies eat the nectar of flowers. Some insects eat other insects. Ladybugs eat aphids. Ant lions eat ants.

   A. Ladybugs eat aphids.

   B. Insects eat different things.

   C. Butterflies eat nectar.

3. Insects live in different kinds of homes. Bees build hives out of wax. Ants and termites build hills on the ground. Some insects, like mayflies and damselflies, live underwater. Other insects live under rocks or in old logs.

   A. Insects live in different kinds of homes.

   B. Some insects live underwater.

   C. Some insects build hills.

Noah's Tadpoles

Read each paragraph. Then, circle the main idea.

1. It was spring. The breeze was soft and warm. The grass on the hills was green. White clouds floated across the blue sky.

   A. The grass was green.

   B. The sky was blue.

   C. It was spring.

2. Noah went outside to play. His ball rolled near the fish pond. Noah had not looked at the pond since fall. He stopped to see the fish. There were four goldfish. There were also some new fish. They were small and dark. Noah ran back to his house to get his dad.

   A. Noah liked to play ball.

   B. Noah saw new fish in the pond.

   C. Noah had four goldfish.

3. Noah's dad came out to look at the new fish. He said they were not fish at all. He said they were tadpoles. He told Noah that the tadpoles would grow bigger and bigger. He said that in a month or two, they would grow legs. The tadpoles would grow up to be frogs.

   A. The new fish were tadpoles.

   B. The tadpoles would grow legs.

   C. Noah's dad put new fish in the pond.

33

Leapfrog Addition

Color the lily pads that have a sum of 12 yellow.

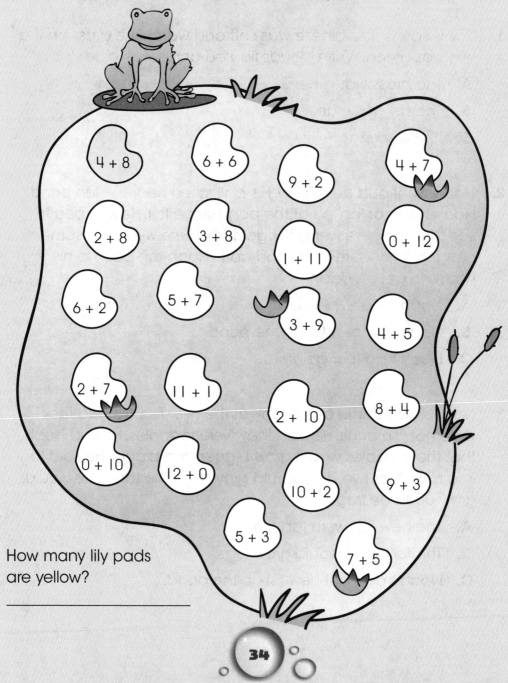

$4 + 8$

$6 + 6$

$9 + 2$

$4 + 7$

$2 + 8$

$3 + 8$

$1 + 11$

$0 + 12$

$6 + 2$

$5 + 7$

$3 + 9$

$4 + 5$

$2 + 7$

$11 + 1$

$2 + 10$

$8 + 4$

$0 + 10$

$12 + 0$

$10 + 2$

$9 + 3$

$5 + 3$

$7 + 5$

How many lily pads
are yellow?

_____

Column Addition

Add the first two numbers. Then, add the sum
of the first two to the last number.

4 + 2 = 6
6 + 5 = 11

$$\begin{array}{r} 4 \\ 2 \\ + 5 \\ \hline \end{array} \quad \begin{array}{r} 6 \\ + 5 \\ \hline 11 \end{array}$$

Study the example above. Then, solve each problem.

1.

5	2	8	6	4
1	2	8	5	4
+ 8	+ 3	+ 2	+ 1	+ 4

2.

7	3	10	6	5
2	6	3	4	8
+ 3	+ 9	+ 3	+ 6	+ 4

3.

3	4	3	1	5
2	3	3	9	7
+ 3	+ 5	+ 3	+ 8	+ 6

4.

2	4	7	6	3
5	2	2	3	2
+ 2	+ 6	+ 4	+ 7	+ 5

Two- and Three- Digit Addition

To find the sum of **2-digit numbers,** add the ones column. Then, add the tens column.	To find the sum of **3-digit numbers,** add the ones column. Then, add the tens column. Last, add the hundreds column.
3 **6** 3 6	3 7 **2** 3 7 2 3 7 2
+ 2 3 + 2 3	+ 6 1 4 + 6 1 4 + 6 1 4
9 5 9	**6** 8 6 9 8 6

Who has the most money? Study the examples above. Then, solve each problem. Color each sum on the piggy banks. The first bank to be completely filled in is the winner.

1.

516	641	523	602
+ 22	+ 341	+ 311	+ 135

2.

221	414	496
+ 425	+ 315	+ 500

3.

814	581	623	203
+ 72	+ 102	+ 311	+ 272

475	982
834	683
729	886

934	538
996	646
737	519

Greater Than, Less Than

Study the examples on page 36. Then, solve each problem. Write
> or < in each circle to compare the sums.

1.
$$\begin{array}{r} 213 \\ + 450 \\ \hline \end{array} \bigcirc \begin{array}{r} 372 \\ + 614 \\ \hline \end{array} \qquad \begin{array}{r} 25 \\ + 51 \\ \hline \end{array} \bigcirc \begin{array}{r} 36 \\ + 41 \\ \hline \end{array}$$

2.
$$\begin{array}{r} 485 \\ + 114 \\ \hline \end{array} \bigcirc \begin{array}{r} 324 \\ + 201 \\ \hline \end{array} \qquad \begin{array}{r} 111 \\ + 74 \\ \hline \end{array} \bigcirc \begin{array}{r} 546 \\ + 201 \\ \hline \end{array}$$

3.
$$\begin{array}{r} 405 \\ + 252 \\ \hline \end{array} \bigcirc \begin{array}{r} 311 \\ + 665 \\ \hline \end{array} \qquad \begin{array}{r} 402 \\ + 417 \\ \hline \end{array} \bigcirc \begin{array}{r} 612 \\ + 281 \\ \hline \end{array}$$

4.
$$\begin{array}{r} 533 \\ + 266 \\ \hline \end{array} \bigcirc \begin{array}{r} 421 \\ + 341 \\ \hline \end{array} \qquad \begin{array}{r} 78 \\ + 11 \\ \hline \end{array} \bigcirc \begin{array}{r} 30 \\ + 50 \\ \hline \end{array}$$

5.
$$\begin{array}{r} 409 \\ + 90 \\ \hline \end{array} \bigcirc \begin{array}{r} 356 \\ + 231 \\ \hline \end{array} \qquad \begin{array}{r} 520 \\ + 307 \\ \hline \end{array} \bigcirc \begin{array}{r} 273 \\ + 514 \\ \hline \end{array}$$

Gorillas

A **fact** is something that you know is true. An **opinion** is what you believe about something.

Gorillas live in the mountains and forests of Zaire, in Africa. Because they are peaceful animals, scientists can study them. Scientists found that gorillas live in groups made up of several females, their babies, and one or more males. A baby gorilla does not live with its mother long. After three years, it sets off on its own. That seems like a short time. Each evening, gorillas build nests to sleep in by picking leaves and laying down on them. Gorillas eat foods that include fruits, leaves, and juicy stems. They probably enjoy their food. Gorillas are becoming extinct because their forests are being destroyed. Many people are trying to save these forests and mountains. We should help save these forests and mountains, too!

Write three facts from the passage.

1. _____

2. _____

3. _____

Write three opinions from the passage.

4. _____

5. _____

6. _____

A Whale of a Tale

Color the facts green and the opinions blue.

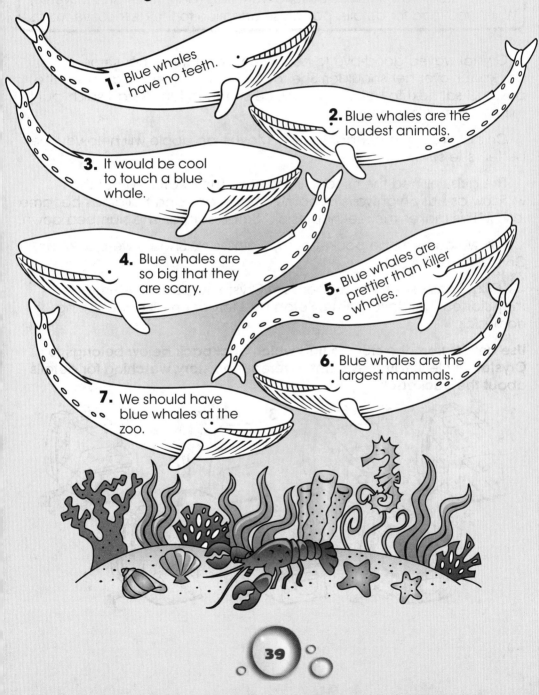

1. Blue whales have no teeth.

2. Blue whales are the loudest animals.

3. It would be cool to touch a blue whale.

4. Blue whales are so big that they are scary.

5. Blue whales are prettier than killer whales.

6. Blue whales are the largest mammals.

7. We should have blue whales at the zoo.

Crystal's Backpack

Some details are written as descriptive words (adjectives and adverbs). When you read for details, pay close attention to the descriptive words.

Crystal waved good-bye to her parents and threw her striped backpack over her shoulder. She found her best friend, Sarah, on the bus and sat next to her. "Camp will be so much fun," Sarah said, "but I think I will miss my family."

Crystal unzipped her backpack. "Maybe an apple will help you feel better," she said.

The girls finished their snack in no time. They watched out the window as busy highways became small roads and buildings became lakes. "This makes me feel homesick," Sarah said as she slumped down.

"I have cards in the pocket of my backpack. Should we play?" Crystal asked.

"Okay," answered Sarah. She beat Crystal twice. By the time they started their third game, Sarah had forgotten all about being homesick.

Use details from the story to find which backpack below belongs to Crystal. Circle it. You may want to reread the story, watching for details about the backpack.

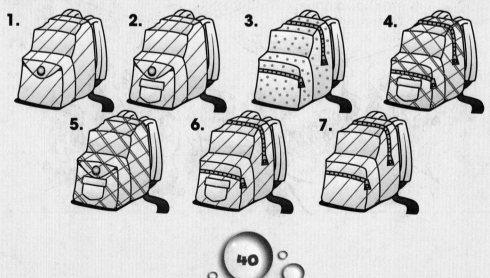

1. 2. 3. 4.

5. 6. 7.

Josh and the Bear

Read the story. Circle *True* if a sentence is true. Circle *False* if it is false.

Josh heard something outside in the woods. It was still dark. Ma and Pa were sleeping. Josh lit the candle by his bed. There was no window in the little cabin. Josh went to the front door and looked out. Little dark eyes looked back at him. The little dark eyes were part of a big, dark face.

Slam! Josh shut the door. He put the big wooden bar across it.

He ran over to the bed and shook his father. "Pa," he said. "Hurry! Bear!" He was too scared to say anything else.

Ma and Pa sat up in bed. Suddenly, they heard a polite knock on the door. Then, the bear began to sing. Josh peeked through the keyhole. He saw the bear juggling four apples.

1. Josh was afraid.   True   False
2. The thing at the door was a mountain lion.   True   False
3. Josh closed the door and put a wooden bar across it. True   False
4. Josh was awake before Pa.   True   False
5. This story could have taken place a long time ago.   True   False
6. The story takes place at noon.   True   False
7. The story is real.   True   False

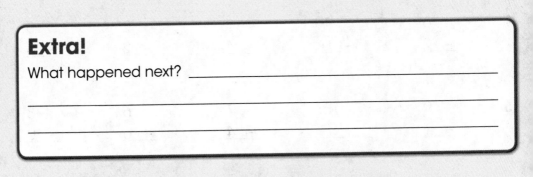

Extra!
What happened next? _____

_____

_____

Subtraction Facts 0-10

Here are 7 dogs. Three dogs go home. Four dogs stay. The mathematical way to write this is **7 – 3 = 4.** This is called a **subtraction equation.**

Study the example above. Then, solve each problem.

1.
$$10 - 1$$ $$4 - 4$$ $$6 - 0$$ $$9 - 6$$ $$8 - 2$$

2.
$$5 - 4$$ $$2 - 1$$ $$5 - 2$$ $$10 - 4$$ $$7 - 3$$

3.
$$10 - 8$$ $$7 - 2$$ $$6 - 3$$ $$9 - 3$$ $$10 - 6$$

4.
$$6 - 2$$ $$1 - 0$$ $$5 - 4$$ $$2 - 2$$ $$5 - 3$$

5.
$$9 - 1$$ $$10 - 5$$ $$7 - 4$$ $$6 - 6$$ $$8 - 0$$

Two-Digit Subtraction

First, subtract the ones column.	Then, subtract the tens column.
5 9 − 2 6 ___ 3	5 9 − 2 6 ___ 3 3

Study the example above. Then, solve each problem.

1.
```
    24        64        83        46        87
  - 14      - 24      - 32      - 15      - 32
```

2.
```
    98        32        57        75        29
  - 84      - 12      - 34      - 62      - 19
```

3.
```
    59        18        80        37        66
  - 53      -  2      - 30      - 14      - 22
```

4.
```
    27        72        33        45        39
  - 24      - 21      - 20      -  5      - 17
```

More Two-Digit Subtraction

Study the example on page 43. Then, solve each problem.

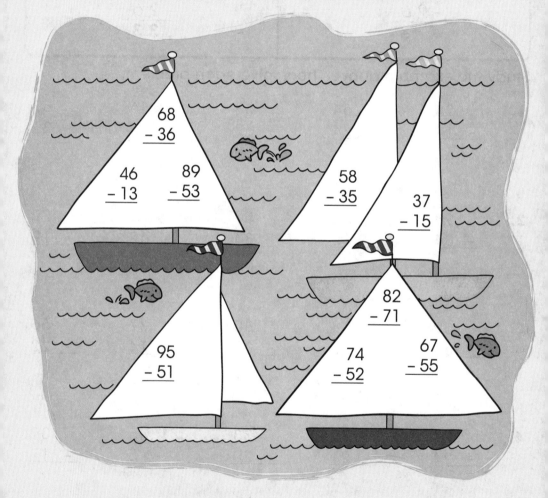

68
− 36

46
− 13

89
− 53

58
− 35

37
− 15

95
− 51

82
− 71

74
− 52

67
− 55

Three-Digit Subtraction

Solving a subtraction problem is the same, no matter how many digits are in the problem.

Study the example on page 43. Then, solve each problem.

YOU MADE IT!

$$849 - 327$$

$$643 - 202$$

$$542 - 311$$

$$747 - 316$$

$$859 - 322$$

$$738 - 527$$

$$698 - 426$$

$$547 - 326$$

$$496 - 182$$

START

Is It Real?

Some stories are about things that can really happen. These are **reality** stories. Some stories are about things that could not really happen. These are **fantasy** stories.

Color the blocks that could be fact yellow. Color the blocks that are fantasy green.

1. Once upon a time, there was a princess named Anna.	**2.** One day, Anna lost her favorite ball in the lake.	**3.** She started to cry. Suddenly, a frog jumped out of the lake.	**4.** "Hello," he said. "I'll get your ball if you promise to take me home."
5. Anna agreed. The frog jumped in and threw the ball to her.	**6.** "Now I can return to the castle with you," the frog said.	**7.** Princess Anna laughed and ran back to the palace without the frog.	**8.** The frog was angry that Anna had broken her promise.
9. The frog went to the palace and knocked on the door.	**10.** The frog told the king how Anna had broken her promise.	**11.** The king said to Anna, "You must always keep your promises."	**12.** So the frog ate dinner from Anna's plate. "Yummy," he said.
13. Then, the frog put on his pajamas and jumped into bed.	**14.** Anna began to cry. Suddenly, the frog turned into a prince.	**15.** Anna and the prince became friends.	**16.** Anna learned to always keep her promises.

Fantastic Facts

By changing something that could really happen into something that could not really happen, you can change reality into fantasy.

Write the next sentence for each story idea, and turn it into fantasy.

1. The clock struck midnight.

_____

_____

2. My dog had been playing in the mud!

_____

_____

3. I looked in my desk at school.

_____

_____

4. The girl looked more closely at the butterfly.

_____

_____

47

Does It Belong?

To help you find the thing that does not belong in a group, look for what the others have in common.
Example: ball, doll, puzzle, pencil (The pencil does not fit because it is not a toy.)

Cross out the word that does not belong in each group.

1.	2.	3.	4.
apple	whale	boat	boots
banana	bobcat	car	hat
potato	squirrel	airplane	mittens
watermelon	raccoon	road	snowman

5.	6.	7.	8.
towel	cotton	candle	bitter
soap	rock	flashlight	sour
shampoo	pillow	mirror	lemon
shoes	feather	lantern	sweet

9.	10.	11.	12.
star	piano	maple	wagon
moon	drum	rose	sled
rocket	song	daisy	scooter
planet	guitar	sunflower	bike

Extra!

Go outside or look out a window. Make a list of 15 things you see outside. Then, divide the list into 3 groups. Give each group a name.

My Day

Classify your day into three groups: morning, afternoon, and evening. Write three activities that belong in each group.

My Morning

1. _____
2. _____
3. _____

My Afternoon

4. _____
5. _____
6. _____

My Evening

7. _____
8. _____
9. _____

49

Addition with Regrouping

First, add the ones column. If the total is more than 9, regroup to the tens column.

```
  1
  2 8
+ 1 3
─────
    1
```

Then, add the tens column.

```
  1
  2 8
+ 1 3
─────
  4 1
```

Study the example above. Then, solve each problem. Remember to regroup.

1. 12 is _____ ten _____ ones

2. 16 is _____ ten _____ ones

3. 14 is _____ ten _____ ones

4. 10 is _____ ten _____ ones

5.
```
□         □         □         □
  35        24        52        73
+ 26      + 68      + 19      + 18
```

6.
```
□         □         □         □
  27        34        22        45
+ 56      + 49      + 59      + 38
```

50

Addition with Regrouping Practice

Study the example on page 50. Then, solve each problem.
Remember to regroup to the tens column.

1.
```
  58      41      66      55      27      24
+ 28    + 29    + 15    +  8    +  9    + 18
```

2.
```
  35      18      46      87      14      62
+ 27    + 23    + 14    +  5    + 19    + 18
```

3.
```
  68      47      65      16      56      19
+ 28    + 47    + 28    + 17    + 29    + 32
```

4.
```
  27      15      19      29      35      58
+ 13    + 69    + 55    + 19    + 46    + 13
```

Regrouping Larger Numbers

Remember, regrouping with three digits is the same as regrouping with two digits. Just keep regrouping across the problem from right to left.

Study the example on page 50. Then, solve each problem.

1.
245	552	368	163	472	224
+ 129	+ 164	+ 167	+ 329	+ 518	+ 538

2.
146	458	173	239	824	569
+ 693	+ 227	+ 281	+ 126	+ 129	+ 146

3.
80	564	439	574	640	267
+ 350	+ 338	+ 127	+ 17	+ 196	+ 181

4.
675	136	805	676	598	129
+ 19	+ 129	+ 66	+ 7	+ 41	+ 89

Addition Riddle

Study the example on page 50. Then, solve each problem. Use the code to answer the riddle.

245 R + 429	617 E + 306	532 K + 428	546 B + 29
385 L + 107	218 S + 145	439 M + 449	374 D + 206
708 V + 59	274 A + 316	137 P + 507	268 C + 528

What cake is as hard as a rock?

$\overline{888}$ $\overline{590}$ $\overline{674}$ $\overline{575}$ $\overline{492}$ $\overline{923}$

$\overline{796}$ $\overline{590}$ $\overline{960}$ $\overline{923}$

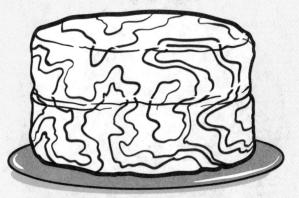

A Real King

> **Characters** are the people, animals, or animated objects in a story. They are brought to life by their actions, and they may even change in the story as people do in real life.

Larry the Lion had been king of the grasslands for a very long time. But the animals felt that they needed a new king. King Larry had become lazy, mean, and selfish. When King Larry learned of how the animals felt, he set them free and laughed to himself, "They will beg to have me back!" The animals did not beg to have Larry back, and so he moved away.

One lonely day, Larry found a mouse that was balancing on a branch over the river. He helped the mouse to the shore. Later, Larry found a baby zebra who was lost. Larry was kind and helped the little zebra find his home.

When the animals learned of Larry's kind acts, they asked him to become their king again. They needed a helpful and strong king, which Larry now seemed to be. King Larry had become a real king!

Complete the lists below by writing three words to describe King Larry at the beginning of the story. Then, write three words to describe King Larry at the end of the story.

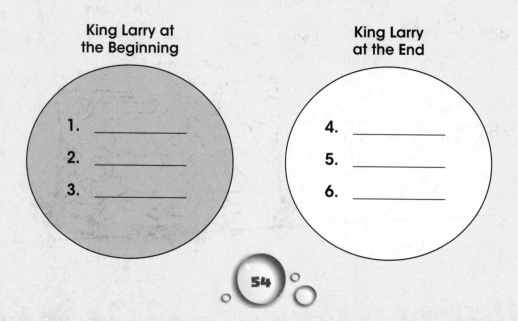

**King Larry at
the Beginning**

1. _____

2. _____

3. _____

**King Larry
at the End**

4. _____

5. _____

6. _____

Feelings

To make stories more interesting, characters often face issues that can be good or bad. A character shows feelings by what he or she says or does.

Each of the children below feels a certain way. Read each sign for clues. Use the words from the word bank to complete the signs. You will not use all of the words.

scared   proud   worried   disappointed   excited

1.
I watched a movie about ghosts last night. Now, I feel _____ .

2.
I forgot my backpack on the bus. I'm _____ about getting it back.

3.
I worked hard and spelled every word the correct way on my test. I feel _____ .

4.
I'm so _____ it rained on the day of my big game.

The Gingerbread Boy

Read the story below.

One day, a woman decided to bake gingerbread into the shape of a boy. She placed raisins for eyes and licorice for the mouth. She used cinnamon candies for the buttons on his vest. When she was satisfied, she popped her little gingerbread boy into the oven. Soon, she could smell the delicious scent of warm gingerbread. She opened the oven door, and the little gingerbread boy popped out.

"Yum! You smell delicious," sighed the old woman.

"Run, run, as fast as you can. You can't catch me. I'm too fast, you see!" the gingerbread boy laughed, and he ran away.

"Oh my!" screamed the old woman, and she ran after her little gingerbread boy.

The little gingerbread boy came to a young boy. "Yum! You smell delicious!" shouted the boy.

But, the gingerbread boy just laughed and said, "Run, run, as fast as you can. You can't catch me. I'm too fast, you see!" And the little gingerbread boy ran away with the old woman and the boy close behind.

The little gingerbread boy came to a girl. "Yum! You smell delicious!" squealed the girl.

But the gingerbread boy just laughed and said, "Run, run, as fast as you can. You can't catch me. I'm too fast, you see!" The gingerbread boy ran away with the old woman, the boy, and the girl close behind.

Soon, the gingerbread boy came to a man. "Yum! You smell delicious!" bellowed the man.

But the gingerbread boy just laughed and said, "Run, run, as fast as you can. You can't catch me. I'm too fast, you see!" And the gingerbread boy ran away with the old woman, the boy, the girl, and the man close behind.

Soon, the gingerbread boy came to a river. "Oh dear," said the gingerbread boy. "How will I cross this river?"

"I'll give you a ride," snickered an alligator with a sly smile. "Just jump on my back."

The gingerbread boy accepted the alligator's offer. As you might expect, the gingerbread boy didn't make it across the river, but instead made it into the belly of the alligator.

When the old woman, the boy, the girl, and the man reached the river, they knew immediately what had happened. "Let's go home," sighed the old woman. "I will make some gingerbread for us. Just a plain loaf of gingerbread."

The Gingerbread Boy

After reading "The Gingerbread Boy," answer the following questions.

1. Number the sentences to show the order in which they happened in the story.

    ___ The old woman baked a plain loaf of gingerbread.

    ___ The old woman chased the gingerbread boy.

    ___ The old woman cut her gingerbread into the shape of a boy.

    ___ The boy chased the gingerbread boy.

    ___ The alligator ate the gingerbread boy.

    ___ The girl chased the gingerbread boy.

    ___ The man chased the gingerbread boy.

    ___ The gingerbread boy came to a river.

2. Find six words that were used in place of the word *said* in the story.

    _____   _____

    _____   _____

    _____   _____

Read the recipe card below. Then, answer the questions.

> **Gingerbread Cookies**
>
> 1 cup molasses
> ½ cup brown sugar
> ⅓ cup water
> ⅓ cup shortening
> 6 cups flour
>
> 1 tsp. baking soda
> 2 tsp. ginger
> 1 tsp. cinnamon
> 1 tsp. all spice
>
> 1. Mix together the molasses, brown sugar, water, and shortening.
> 2. Sift together flour, soda, and spices. Then, add to molasses mixture. Cover and refrigerate overnight.
> 3. Heat oven to 350°F. Roll out dough on a floured board. Use cookie cutters to cut shapes. Place cookies on a cookie sheet. Bake 10–12 minutes.
>
> Makes 2 dozen cookies.

3. How many cups of flour will you need? _____

4. How hot should the oven be?

    _____

5. How long do you need to bake the cookies?

    _____

6. How many cookies will this recipe make?

    _____

Subtraction with Regrouping

First, subtract the ones column.	You cannot subtract 8 from 1. To regroup, borrow 1 ten from the tens column. Add it to the ones column. Subtract the ones column.	Last, subtract the tens column.
6 1 − 2 8	⁵⁄₆¹1 − 2 8 3	⁵⁄₆¹1 − 2 8 3 3

Study the example above. Then, solve each problem.

1.　36　　33　　51　　53　　84
　　− 17　− 14　− 34　− 24　− 27

2.　85　　64　　67　　30　　34
　　− 26　− 18　− 29　− 18　− 17

3.　61　　43　　20　　35　　43
　　− 32　− 34　− 12　− 16　− 28

4.　83　　52　　63　　77　　66
　　− 55　− 35　− 26　− 38　− 48

Subtraction with Regrouping Practice

Study the example on page 58. Then, solve each problem.

1.
$$\begin{array}{r} 64 \\ -\ 18 \\ \hline \end{array}$$
$$\begin{array}{r} 52 \\ -\ 16 \\ \hline \end{array}$$
$$\begin{array}{r} 94 \\ -\ 36 \\ \hline \end{array}$$
$$\begin{array}{r} 81 \\ -\ 74 \\ \hline \end{array}$$

2.
$$\begin{array}{r} 70 \\ -\ 59 \\ \hline \end{array}$$
$$\begin{array}{r} 48 \\ -\ 29 \\ \hline \end{array}$$
$$\begin{array}{r} 66 \\ -\ 38 \\ \hline \end{array}$$
$$\begin{array}{r} 96 \\ -\ 19 \\ \hline \end{array}$$

3.
$$\begin{array}{r} 41 \\ -\ 27 \\ \hline \end{array}$$
$$\begin{array}{r} 84 \\ -\ 36 \\ \hline \end{array}$$
$$\begin{array}{r} 80 \\ -\ 64 \\ \hline \end{array}$$
$$\begin{array}{r} 78 \\ -\ 9 \\ \hline \end{array}$$

Regrouping Larger Numbers

Study the example on page 58. Then, solve each problem.

1.

624	162	609	378	809	236
− 135	− 13	− 319	− 179	− 512	− 129

2.

564	850	269	460	648	133
− 377	− 8	− 94	− 278	− 129	− 24

3.

528	437	644	434	942	519
− 134	− 129	− 246	− 225	− 367	− 287

4.

410	840	864	717	547	933
− 132	− 38	− 239	− 226	− 139	− 199

Subtraction Riddle

Study the example on page 58. Then, solve each problem. Use the code to answer the riddle.

621 P − 283	917 R − 178	438 O − 69	553 H − 286
941 M − 173	864 T − 469	740 L − 97	982 K − 498
616 E − 58	804 U − 193	464 C − 275	623 Y − 458

What dance are the Pilgrims most known for?

$$\overline{395}\ \overline{267}\ \overline{558}$$

$$\overline{338}\ \overline{643}\ \overline{165}\ \overline{768}\ \overline{369}\ \overline{611}\ \overline{395}\ \overline{267}$$

$$\overline{739}\ \overline{369}\ \overline{189}\ \overline{484}$$

Rebecca and Neela

Read the story below. Then, answer the questions.

Rebecca and Neela are best friends. They have the same haircut. They wear the same clothes. They love to read. Both girls have their own pet. Rebecca has a bird. Neela has a mouse. Rebecca lets her bird, Jade, fly around her room. Neela keeps her mouse, Julius, in his cage. Rebecca and Neela take good care of their pets.

1. What do Rebecca and Neela love to do? _____

2. How do the girls look alike? _____
   _____

3. What is different about the girls? _____
   _____

4. How do they play differently with their pets? _____
   _____

Alligators & Crocodiles

Read the passage below.

Is that a log in the water? It doesn't seem to be moving. But, are those eyes? Watch out! It's an alligator! Or is it a crocodile? Many people confuse alligators and crocodiles. They look and act very much the same.

Alligators and crocodiles live in the water. They eat fish, turtles, birds, and other animals. Crocodiles have pointed snouts. Alligators have wide, rounded snouts. The upper jaw of the alligator is wider than its lower jaw. When its mouth is closed, most of its teeth are hidden. The upper and lower jaws of the crocodile are about the same size. Many of its teeth can be seen when its mouth is closed.

Crocodiles and alligators are cold-blooded. Cold-blooded animals stay cool in the water and warm in the sun. Alligators prefer to live in fresh water. Crocodiles are often found in salt water.

People may think that alligators and crocodiles are slow because they lie so still in the water. But, they can move fast on land with their short legs. Both animals are fierce. Stay away! They can be dangerous.

Alligators & Crocodiles

Complete the Venn diagram to describe alligators and crocodiles. Use the phrases in the Fact Bank.

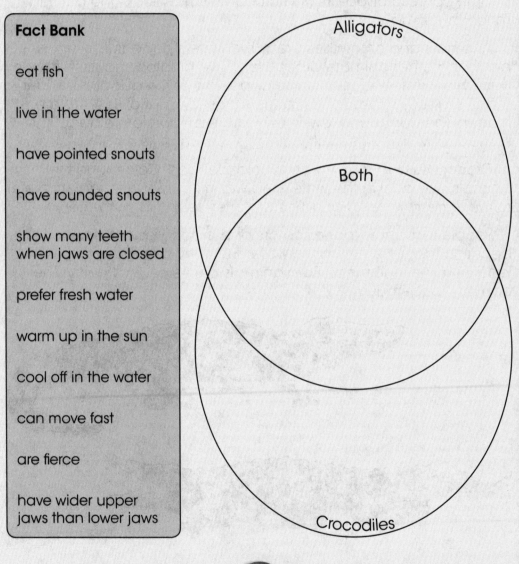

Fact Bank

eat fish

live in the water

have pointed snouts

have rounded snouts

show many teeth
when jaws are closed

prefer fresh water

warm up in the sun

cool off in the water

can move fast

are fierce

have wider upper
jaws than lower jaws

Alligators

Both

Crocodiles

Super Sport

> **Sequencing** means putting events from a story in the order that they happened.

Read "Super Sport." Then, read the sentences below. Write a number in front of each sentence to show the order in which they happened.

In December 1891, at McGill University in Springfield, MA, Dr. James Naismith nailed a peach basket onto a 10-foot pole. In order to keep his students occupied and healthy during the long New England winters, he created a new indoor game that would later be named basketball.

In 1892, Senda Berenson, a physical education teacher at Smith College, modified Naismith's rules so that her female students could play the new game.

The first official basketball game was played in a YMCA gymnasium on January 20, 1892. The game had nine players and was on a court half the size of today's standard court.

The National Basketball Association (NBA) was formed in 1946 with 11 teams. The first game was played on November 1, 1946, between the Toronto Huskies and the New York Knickerbockers. The Women's National Basketball Association (WNBA) began in 1997 with eight teams. The first season began on June 21, 1997.

____ The National Basketball Association was formed.

____ Dr. James Naismith created a new game for his students.

____ The first official basketball game was played.

____ The Women's National Basketball association began.

____ Senda Berenson modified the game for her female students.

____ The Toronto Huskies played the New York Knickerbockers.

What Time Is It?

The short hand is called the **hour** hand. It tells the hour. The long hand is called the **minute** hand. It tells the minutes. This clock shows 30 minutes past 9 o'clock. It shows 9:30.

Study the example above. Then, circle the correct time for each clock.

1.

3:00   3:30   12:00

2.

2:30   3:30   1:30

3.

7:00   7:30   8:30

4.

6:00   12:30   12:00

5.

11:00   12:00   10:00

6.

12:00   12:30   6:00

Drawing Hands on Clocks

Study the example on page 66. Then, draw the hands on each clock to show the time.

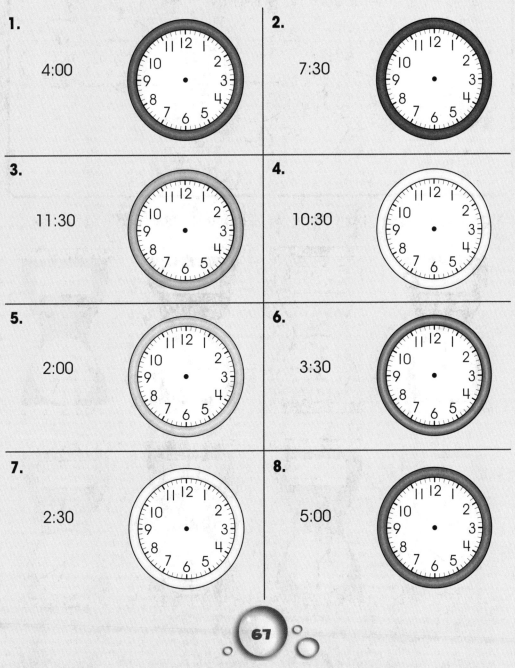

1.

4:00

2.

7:30

3.

11:30

4.

10:30

5.

2:00

6.

3:30

7.

2:30

8.

5:00

Telling Time in Five-Minute Intervals

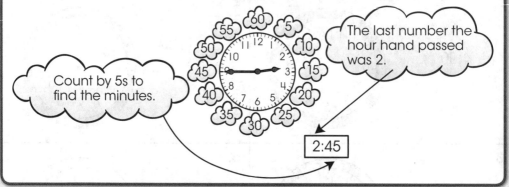

The short hand on a clock tells the hour. Always use the last number that the hour hand passed.

Count by 5s to find the minutes.

The last number the hour hand passed was 2.

2:45

Study the example above. Then, write the time shown on each clock.

1.

2.

Writing Time

Time can be written or said in different ways.

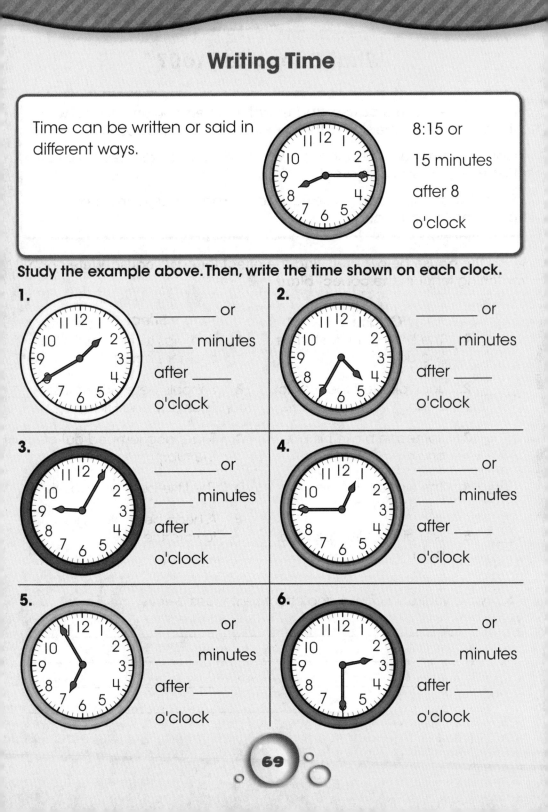

8:15 or

15 minutes

after 8

o'clock

Study the example above. Then, write the time shown on each clock.

1.

_____ or

_____ minutes

after _____

o'clock

2.

_____ or

_____ minutes

after _____

o'clock

3.

_____ or

_____ minutes

after _____

o'clock

4.

_____ or

_____ minutes

after _____

o'clock

5.

_____ or

_____ minutes

after _____

o'clock

6.

_____ or

_____ minutes

after _____

o'clock

What Does It Tell You?

Many stories have a **cause and effect** that help you understand why things happen in the stories. Think about the story "Little Red Riding Hood."

Cause (what made it happen): It was really the wolf dressed up as Little Red Riding Hood's grandma!

Effect (what happened): Little Red Riding Hood thought that her grandma looked strange.

Read the cause below. Then, find the effect for each cause. Write each matching letter in the correct blank.

Cause	**Effect**
_____ **1.** The snowstorm lasted for two days.	**A.** Two pigs ran to their brother's house.
_____ **2.** Jack planted the magic beans.	**B.** Schools were closed last Thursday and Friday.
_____ **3.** Someone broke his little chair.	**C.** Tara's dog jumped out of the tub.
_____ **4.** The wolf blew their houses down.	**D.** The little bear was upset.
_____ **5.** She did not like taking a bath.	**E.** A huge bean stalk grew toward the sky.

6. Write your own cause and effect sentences below.

_____

_____

_____

_____

70

April's Song

Read the story below.

April was excited to try out for the play. For weeks and weeks she practiced all of her lines in front of a mirror. The play had two main parts: a deer and a butterfly. April wanted the part of the butterfly.

Tryouts were on Friday. Thursday night, April had a hard time getting to sleep. "What if I forget my lines?" she asked herself. Finally, Friday arrived. After lunch, all of the students who wanted to try out for the play were asked to go to the auditorium. Sally went first. She wanted to be the deer. She did a great job. April hoped that she would do as well as Sally. Next, it was Albert's turn. He was trying out for the part of the butterfly. Albert did a great job, too. Then, it was April's turn. She walked onto the stage. Mrs. Johnson, the music teacher, asked her to say her lines. April was speechless. She could not say a word. Her mouth was dry, and she felt sick. April had stage fright!

When April got home, she cried as she told her parents what happened. Her mother said that when she was a little girl, she was afraid to talk in front of people, too. April was relieved that she was not the only person with stage fright.

The next day, Mrs. Johnson gave out parts in the play. Sally got the part of the deer. Albert got the part of the butterfly. April's part was a violet. After all of her practicing, April would be a flower in the school play. She was very disappointed.

April's main job was to hold a welcome sign at the edge of the stage. She did not have any lines. Even though her grandmother made her a beautiful violet costume, April was not excited when it was time for the play. "Why do I have to go?" she asked her parents. "All of the other kids have lines. The audience will laugh at me." April's parents reminded her that all of the parts in the play were important.

April's Song

On the night of the play, April went to her place on stage early. She decided that she would be the best violet the school had ever seen. She smiled throughout the play. At the end of the play, Allison, the narrator, was supposed to come onto the stage and thank everyone for coming. However, Allison was nowhere to be found!

Out of the corner of her eye, April noticed Mrs. Johnson waving at her. She was trying to tell her something. April realized that Mrs. Johnson was trying to tell her to thank the audience. Before she realized what she was doing, April began singing out loud. She was singing, "Good night, thank you for coming. Good night, we hope you enjoyed the show. Good night, we thank you all for coming. Good night, it's time for you to go!"

Everyone clapped and cheered. They loved April's song! It was a wonderful way to end the play. Mrs. Johnson thought that April did such a great job, she asked her to sing the same ending for the other shows.

April realized that when she sang on stage, she was not as frightened as when she tried to talk. She ended each show with her song, and even added a dance for the last performance. Being a flower was not a bad thing after all.

April's Song

After reading "April's Song," answer the following questions.

1. What part did April want in the play?
   - **A.** the violet
   - **B.** the deer
   - **C.** the butterfly
   - **D.** the narrator

2. Why didn't April get the part she wanted?
   - **A.** She yelled her lines.
   - **B.** She had stage fright.
   - **C.** She did not practice for her part.
   - **D.** She sang her lines instead of speaking.

3. Why wasn't April excited on the night of the play?
   - **A.** She did not like her costume.
   - **B.** She did not know her lines.
   - **C.** She was mad at Sally and Albert.
   - **D.** She thought that people would laugh at her.

4. Why did Mrs. Johnson wave at April?
   - **A.** She wanted April to thank the audience.
   - **B.** She wanted April to smile for the camera.
   - **C.** She wanted to say hello to April.
   - **D.** She was trying to tell April to hold up her sign.

Adding Coins

To count how much money you have, add the coins together.

50¢   25¢   10¢

5¢   1¢

25 + 25 + 25 = 75¢

Study the coin values and the example above. Then, count the coins in each problem. Write how much money is shown.

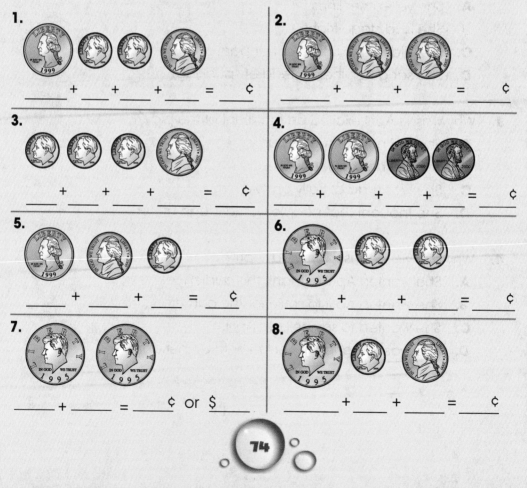

1.

_____ + _____ + _____ + _____ = _____ ¢

2.

_____ + _____ + _____ = _____ ¢

3.

_____ + _____ + _____ + _____ = _____ ¢

4.

_____ + _____ + _____ + _____ = _____ ¢

5.

_____ + _____ + _____ = _____ ¢

6.

_____ + _____ + _____ = _____ ¢

7.

_____ + _____ = _____ ¢ or $ _____

8.

_____ + _____ + _____ = _____ ¢

How Much Does It Cost?

Study the coin values and the example on page 74. Then, draw a line to match each toy with the amount of money it costs.

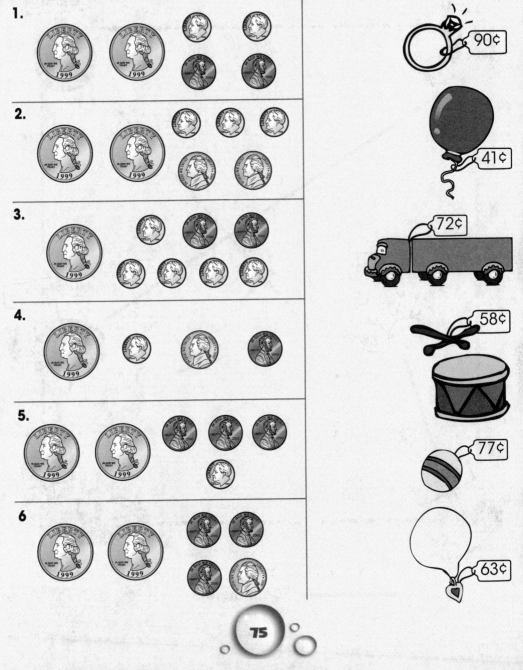

In the Garden

To complete this activity, use the map and map key with page 77.

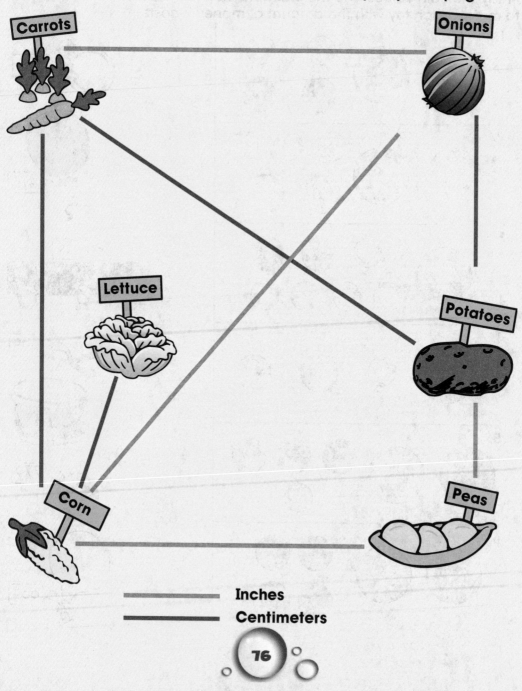

Carrots

Onions

Lettuce

Potatoes

Corn

Peas

_____ Inches

_____ Centimeters

In the Garden

Iggy the Lizard and Slinky the Salamander are feasting in the garden. Measure their paths on page 76. Measure Iggy's path with inches. Iggy's path is the blue line. Measure Slinky's path with centimeters. Slinky's path is the red line. Then, write each length to the nearest inch or centimeter.

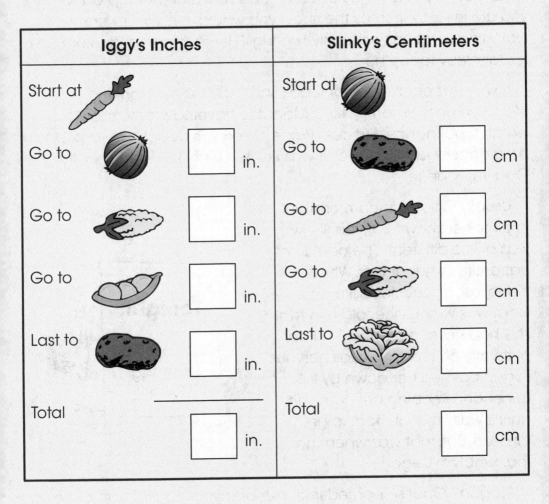

Iggy's Inches		Slinky's Centimeters	
Start at (carrot)		Start at (onion)	
Go to (onion)	___ in.	Go to (potato)	___ cm
Go to (corn)	___ in.	Go to (carrot)	___ cm
Go to (peas)	___ in.	Go to (corn)	___ cm
Last to (potato)	___ in.	Last to (cabbage)	___ cm
Total	___ in.	Total	___ cm

Opal's Dance

Read the story below.

Opal is known throughout the sea as one of the most talented creatures. She has been tap dancing for as long as she can remember. Opal is an octopus. When you watch her tap dance, you are in for four times the show you would see if you were watching someone with only two legs. Her fans come from oceans far, far away to see her.

It was a special night for Opal. She was dancing for King Manatee and his family. King Manatee traveled many miles to watch Opal dance. Princess Paige, the king's daughter, wanted to be a dancer just like Opal. It was Paige's birthday wish to watch Opal tap dance.

Usually, Opal was comfortable in all of her shows. But, this show was a little different. She could not eat a bite of her dinner. When her friend, Logan Lobster, asked her what was wrong, she told him that she had never performed in front of royalty before. Opal was nervous. Logan calmed her down by talking to her and keeping her company until it was time for Opal to get dressed. But, that was when the real problem began.

Tonight:

Tap Dancing Opal

"Logan!" Opal screamed from her dressing room. "There are only seven tap shoes in my closet! I can't find my other shoe!"

Opal's Dance

"Are you sure?" Logan asked. "They were all here last night when you performed for the Tuna family."

"I know," replied Opal. "I can't imagine what happened to that shoe. Oh, what should I do?"

Opal put on her other seven shoes and gave tapping a try in her dressing room. "It's no use," she cried. "We will have to cancel the show.

I can't dance with only seven shoes. It will ruin the rhythm of the routines." Logan went out to break the bad news.

Just after he left, Opal heard a tiny voice. "Maybe I can help," the voice said.

"Who said that?" Opal asked.

"It's me, Callie." Opal looked down to see her neighbor, Callie Clam, peeking into her dressing room door. "I'm tiny, but I have very big ideas," Callie said. Opal listened to Callie's plan.

Just in time, Callie and Opal caught up with Logan. "Don't cancel the show," Opal said. "Callie has a plan, and I think it just might work!"

They shared the idea with Logan. "Let's give it a try," he said.

Opal's Dance

Opal danced better than she had ever danced before. She was given three standing ovations, and on the third, she spoke. "Your majesties, I must tell you what an honor it has been to dance for you. I must also tell you that I did not perform alone tonight." At that moment, Opal took something off of the bottom of one of her tentacles. It was Callie! She continued, "I would like to introduce you to my dear friend, Callie Clam. You see, I couldn't find one of my tap shoes tonight, and Callie had a great idea. She suggested that I tape her to the bottom of one of my regular shoes. Then, she would make a tapping sound just like the other shoes. We tried it, and it worked."

Callie smiled at the princess and said, "It's a pleasure to meet you."

"Likewise," said Princess Paige.

The king was pleased that his daughter's heroine and Callie had been able to demonstrate such teamwork. He decided to do something special for Opal and Callie. The king had a brand new dance studio built for Opal. In the front row, he built a special chair, taller than the rest, for Callie. Every year, the king and his family returned for Paige's birthday, just to watch Opal dance.

Opal's Dance

After reading "Opal's Dance," answer the following questions.

1. Number the sentences to put the events in the correct order.
   __ Opal was given three standing ovations for her show.
   __ Opal couldn't find one of her shoes.
   __ Callie, Opal, and Paige became friends.
   __ Callie had a plan to help Opal.
   __ The king was pleased with Opal and Callie's teamwork.

2. Why was the night in the story a special night for Opal?
   A. It was her birthday.
   B. She and Logan became friends.
   C. She was dancing for King Manatee and his family.
   D. She was singing a new song for the king.

3. How did Callie help Opal?
   A. She brought her dinner on the night of her big show.
   B. She let Opal tape her to her shoe so that the shoe would make a tapping sound.
   C. She helped Opal learn her new dance routine.
   D. She introduced Opal to King Manatee and Princess Paige.

4. What did the king do for Callie?
   A. He came to watch Opal dance every year.
   B. He built a new dance studio.
   C. He took everyone out to dinner.
   D. He built her a special tall chair in the front row of the new dance studio.

5. What do you think happened to Opal's shoe?

   _____

   _____

81

Introduction to Fractions

A **fraction** tells how many parts of a whole.
The top number tells how many parts are shaded.
The bottom number tells how many parts in all.

parts shaded ➡️ $\dfrac{1}{4}$ ⬅️ parts in all

Study the example above. Then, write the correct fraction.

1.

$\dfrac{}{4}$

2.

$\dfrac{}{2}$

3.

$\dfrac{}{4}$

4.

$\dfrac{}{4}$

5.

$\dfrac{}{3}$

6.

$\dfrac{}{3}$

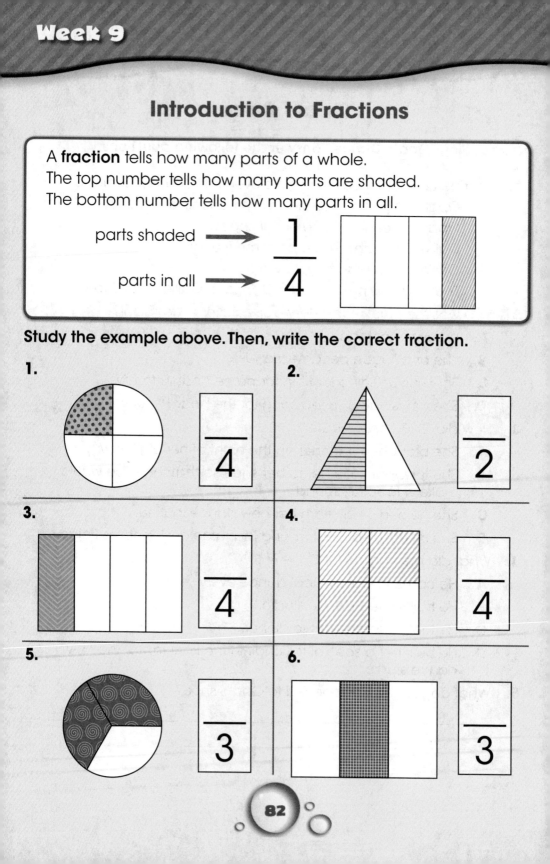

Exploring Fractions

There are 4 **parts,** so the bottom number is 4.
One part is shaded.
The answer is $\frac{1}{4}$.

$\frac{1}{2}$ $\frac{1}{3}$ $\left(\frac{1}{4}\right)$

Study the example above. Then, circle the fraction that tells how much is shaded in each shape.

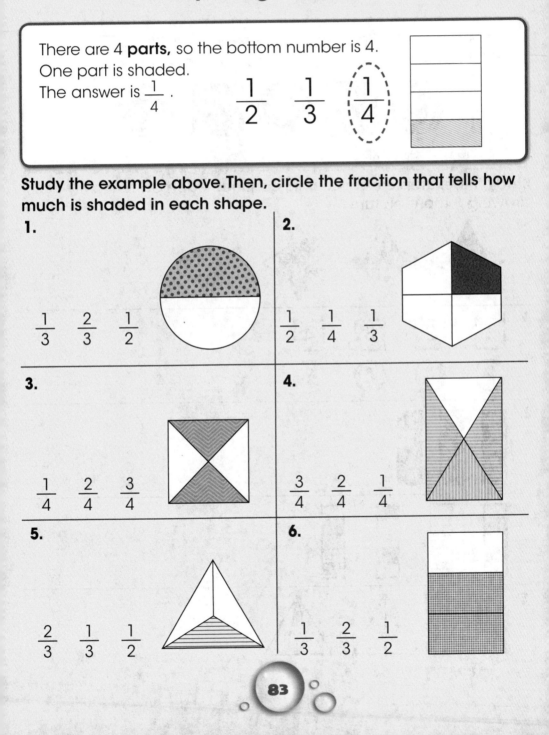

1.

$\frac{1}{3}$ $\frac{2}{3}$ $\frac{1}{2}$

2.

$\frac{1}{2}$ $\frac{1}{4}$ $\frac{1}{3}$

3.

$\frac{1}{4}$ $\frac{2}{4}$ $\frac{3}{4}$

4.

$\frac{3}{4}$ $\frac{2}{4}$ $\frac{1}{4}$

5.

$\frac{2}{3}$ $\frac{1}{3}$ $\frac{1}{2}$

6.

$\frac{1}{3}$ $\frac{2}{3}$ $\frac{1}{2}$

Recognizing Patterns

Patterns are sets of pictures, numbers, or letters that repeat in a certain order. This pattern is circle, square, circle, square.

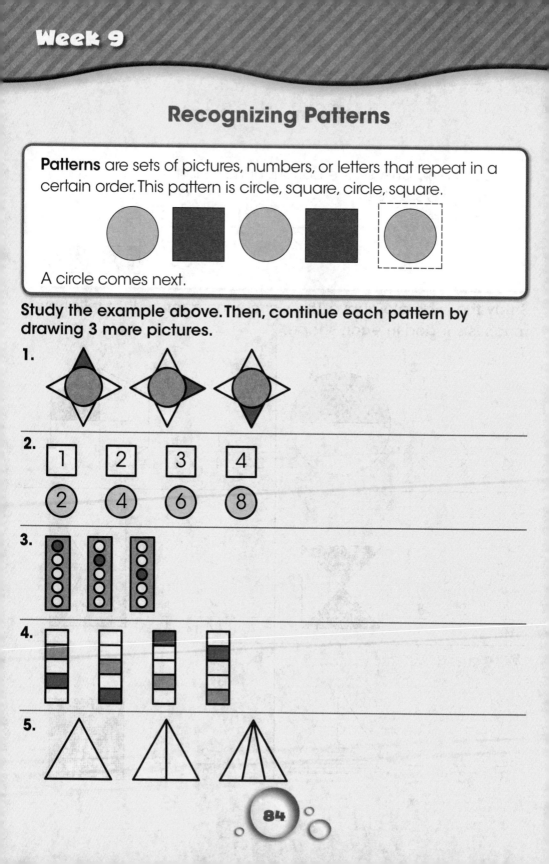

A circle comes next.

Study the example above. Then, continue each pattern by drawing 3 more pictures.

1.

2.

| 1 | 2 | 3 | 4 |

2 4 6 8

3.

4.

5.

Predicting Patterns

To determine a pattern, draw the pattern or think about it. The ninth shape in this pattern will be a square.

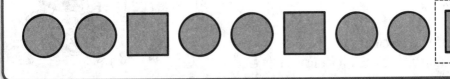

Study the example above. Then, look at each pattern. Draw the shape to answer each question.

1. What will the eighth shape be?

_____

2. What will the tenth shape be?

_____

3. What will the next shape be?

_____

4. What will the seventh shape be?

_____

5. What will the ninth shape be?

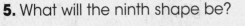

_____

6. What will the tenth shape be?

_____

The Great Race

Find a friend and play this game.

What You Will Need:
Coin
Space Markers

Object of the Game:
To be the first to cross the finish line

How to Play:
The youngest player goes first.
Flip a coin. Move one space for heads. Move two spaces for tails.
Follow the directions on each space.

Start	Slow start. Go back 1 space.	Great start! Go ahead 2 spaces.			Tripped on shoelace. Go back 1 space.	
			Running strong. Take another turn.			←
→	Record time. Go ahead 3 spaces.		Leg cramps. Lose a turn.			
				Getting tired. Go back 3 spaces.		←
→	Missed a hurdle. Go back 2 spaces.					**Finish**

The Great Race

Answer the following questions using the activity on page 86.

1. What is the main idea?
   A. how to play a game
   B. how to run in a race
   C. how to be in first place

2. Who goes first?
   A. the owner of the game
   B. the biggest person
   C. the youngest person

3. What is the object of the game?
   A. to not trip when running a race
   B. to be the first to cross the finish line
   C. to get the best start

4. What is the consequence of each action?
   A. tripped on shoelace

   _____

   B. getting tired

   _____

   C. missed a hurdle

   _____

Read this game box. Answer the questions below.

A Rainbow Bridge Game

Hop to It!

The game that keeps you on your toes

For 3 or more players
For ages 5 to adult

5. What is the game's name?

   _____

6. How old do you need to be to play the game? _____

7. Can two people play the game? _____

Write the base word for the following words:

8. tripped _____

9. running _____

10. getting _____

11. tired _____

12. crossed _____

87

Treasure Map

Ben and Matt were playing pirates. While digging for treasure, they found this map. Follow the directions to find the treasure. Mark an *X* where the treasure is buried.

Start in the Red River Valley.

Go northeast to the Black Forest.

Go northeast to the next forest.

Travel north to the Purple Mountains.

Cross the Red River to the Blue Mountains.

Go south, but do not cross the Red River again.

The treasure is buried here.

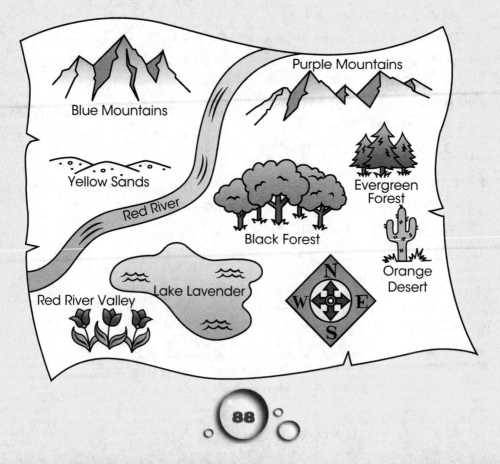

Treasure Map

Answer the following questions using the treasure map on page 88.

1. Where is the treasure buried?

   _____

2. When you go northeast from the Black Forest, what forest do you find?

   _____

3. Draw a line from the color to the place as noted on the map.

   Yellow   Mountains

   Orange   River

   Red   Sands

   Purple   Desert

Write the base word for each word below.

4. playing _____

5. digging _____

6. buried _____

7. missing _____

8. hunting _____

Cross out the word that does not belong in each group.

9. blue   yellow
   red   sky

10. forest   mountains
    tree   desert

11. north   left
    south   east

12. desert   ocean
    river   lake

13. mountain   hill
    leak   valley

14. Draw your own map. Write directions for a friend to follow.

Introduction to Multiplication

Multiplication is the fastest way to add equal groups. Multiplying means adding the same number over and over.

$$2 + 2 + 2$$
3 groups of 2
$$3 \times 2$$
$$6$$

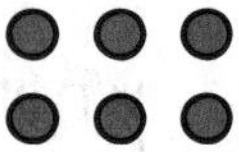

Study the example above. Then, draw the correct number of marbles in each bag. Solve the problem.

1.

4 bags, 2 marbles in each bag
$$4 \times 2 = \underline{\quad}$$

2.

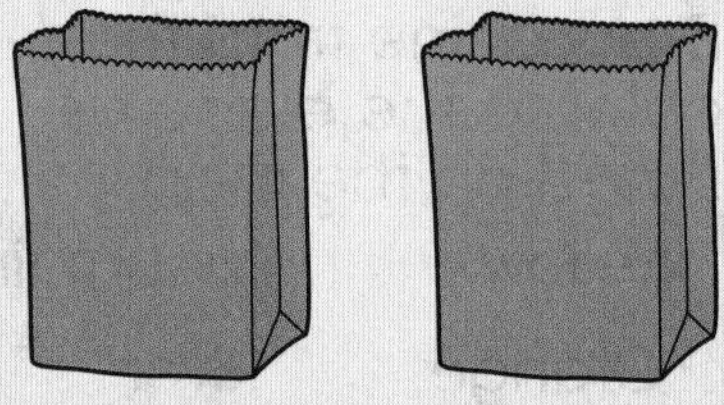

2 bags, 4 marbles in each bag
$$2 \times 4 = \underline{\quad}$$

3.

3 bags, 4 marbles in each bag
$$3 \times 4 = \underline{\quad}$$

4.

4 bags, 3 marbles in each bag
$$4 \times 3 = \underline{\quad}$$

Fishing for Multiplication

The **multiplication sign (x)** means "groups of." 3 x 2 means 3 groups of 2.

Study the example on page 90. Then, draw a line from each multiplication problem to its matching picture.

3 x 3

5 x 1

4 x 2

3 x 2

4 x 1

5 x 2

3 x 1

3 x 4

1.

2.

3.

4.

5.

6.

7.

8.

91

Addition

> **Problem solving** means using the numbers in a story to solve a math problem.
>
> **Example:** John ate 12 grapes. Then, he ate 10 more. How many grapes did he eat in all? 12 + 10 = 22 John ate 22 grapes.

Study the example above. Then, write an addition problem for each story. Find the answer. Label the answer.

1. The school play will have 14 tigers, 6 jaguars, and 16 lions. How many wild cats will there be in all?

2. There are 22 boys and 27 girls in the play. How many total children are in the play?

3. Three dads and 16 moms are making costumes. How many parents are helping altogether?

4. The school sold 132 adult tickets and 68 child tickets. How many tickets did they sell combined?

5. There will be 2 shows on Friday, 2 shows on Saturday, and 1 show on Sunday. How many shows will there be in all?

6. The actors will need 14 hats, 24 coats, and 31 scarves. How many props will they need combined?

Subtraction

There are some key words that tell you to subtract when solving story problems. They are **have left, how many more, how many fewer, how much change,** and **difference.**

Study the example on page 92. Then, use the prices for the snacks below to write each subtraction problem. Find the answer.

$2.38 $1.29 $1.38 $1.34

1. Mr. Smith bought a hot dog during the play. He paid with $3.00. How much change will he get?

2. How much more does popcorn cost than soda?

3. The class sold 26 sodas and 14 cupcakes. How many fewer cupcakes did they sell?

4. Ms. Green bought 10 sodas and 3 hot dogs. How many more sodas did she buy?

5. What is the difference in price between a hot dog and a soda?

6. Erin bought a soda. She paid with $1.50. How much change will she get?

Answer Key

Page 15: 1. A.; **2.** Wash your hands with soap., Cover your mouth when you cough or sneeze., Get plenty of sleep., Eat healthy meals.; **3.** T, F, T; **4.** i; **5.** u; **6.** u; **7.** o; **8.** noun; **9.** Answers will vary.

Page 17: 1. B.; **2.** 4, 1, 3, 2; **3.** B.; **4.** o; **5.** a; **6.** a; **7.** u; **8.** noun; **9.** verb; **10.** noun; **11.** verb; **12.** noun; **13.** verb

Page 18: 1. two; **2.** eight; **3.** one, three; **4.** eleven; **5.** one; **6.** seven, nine; **7.** two, four; **8.** eight, **9.** three; **10.** eleven; **11.** two; **12.** three; **13.** five, seven; **14.** nine; **15.** six

Page 19: HE WAS IN SHOCK

Page 20: 1. 2, 4, 6, 8, 10, 12, 14, 16, 18, 20, 22, 24, 26, 28, 30, 32, 34, 36, 38, 40; **2.** 3, 6, 9, 12, 15, 18, 21, 23, 27, 30, 33, 36, 39; **3.** 15, 21; **4.** 20, 24; **5.** 8, 14; **6.** 3, 12; **7.** 4, 6, 12; **8.** 3, 12, 15

Page 21: 1. yellow: 5, 10, 15, 20, 25, 30, 35, 40, 45, 50, 55, 60, 65, 70, 75, 80, 85, 90, 95, 100; red: 10, 20, 30, 40, 50, 60, 70, 80, 90, 100; **2.** 10, 15; **3.** 50, 60, 100; **4.** 80, 85, 90; **5.** 20, 30, 40, 50; **6.** 35, 40, 55, 60, 65

Page 23: 1. A.; **2.** D.; **3.** B.; **4.** B.; **5.** D.

Page 25: 1. B; **2.** T; **3.** B; **4.** G; **5.** G; **6.** Pictures will vary.; **7.** fraternal; **8.** base, teeth, play, braces, both

Page 26: 1. fourth; **2.** fifth; **3.** second; **4.** first; **5.** sixth; **6.** third; **7.** seventh; **8.** eighth

Page 27: 1. red: 13, 3, 11, 21, 7, 17, 5, 23, 19, 9, 15; yellow: 2, 20, 6, 12, 8, 18, 22, 4, 14, 16, 10; **2.** Denise; **3.** Matt; **4.** Rob; **5.** Allie; **6.** Tanner

Page 28: 1. 5 = triangle, 2 = circle; **2.** 1st 9 = square, 2nd 9 = circle; **3.** 2 = circle, 4 = square, 1 = triangle; **4.** 5 = circle, 6 = triangle; **5.** 3 = square, 1 = crossed out, 7 = circle; **6.** 1st 6 = square, 2nd 6 = crossed out, 2 = triangle; **7.** 4 = circle, 5 = square

Page 29: 1. 1, 2, 9; **2.** 9, 3, 6; **3.** 4, 6, 2; **4.** 2, 4, 8; **5.** 3, 2, 0; **6.** 8, 6, 3; **7.** 264; **8.** 782; **9.** 914; **10.** 153; **11.** 305; **12.** 376

Page 31: 1. The Panda Keeper; **2.** Becoming a Zookeeper; **3.** When Yang Yang Is Sick; **4.** What Yang Yang Eats

Page 32: 1. C.; **2.** B.; **3.** A.

Page 33: 1. C.; **2.** B.; **3.** A.

Page 34: 6 + 6, 1 +11, 0 + 12, 5 + 7, 3 + 9, 11 + 1, 2 + 10, 8 + 4, 12 + 0, 10 + 2, 9 + 3, 7 + 5; 13 lily pads

Page 35: 1. 14, 7, 18, 12, 12; **2.** 12, 18, 16, 16, 17; **3.** 8, 12, 9, 18, 18; **4.** 9, 12, 13, 16, 10

Page 36: 1. 538, 982, 834, 737; **2.** 646, 729, 996; **3.** 886, 683, 934, 475; The left piggy bank is the winner.

Page 37: 1. <, <; **2.** >, <; **3.** <, <; **4.** >, >; **5.** <, >

Page 38: 1. Gorillas live in the mountains and the forests of Zaire; **2.** Gorillas live in groups.; **3.** Each evening, gorillas build nests to sleep in.; **4.** They probably enjoy their food.; **5.** A baby gorilla does not live with its mother long.; **6.** We should help save these forests and mountains.

Page 39: 1. fact; **2.** fact; **3.** opinion; **4.** opinion; **5.** opinion; **6.** fact; **7.** opinion

Page 40: Bookbag 6

Page 41: 1. True; **2.** False; **3.** True; **4.** True; **5.** True; **6.** False; **7.** False; Extra: Answers will vary.

Page 42: 1. 9, 0, 6, 3, 6; **2.** 1, 1, 3, 6, 4; **3.** 2, 5, 3, 6, 4; **4.** 4, 1, 1, 0, 2; **5.** 8, 5, 3, 0, 8

Page 43: 1. 10, 40, 51, 31, 5; **2.** 14, 20, 23, 13, 10; 6, 16, 50, 23, 44; **4.** 3, 1, 13, 40, 22

Page 44: From left to right and top to bottom: 3 – 36 = 32, 46 – 13 = 3, 89 – 53 = 36, 58 – 35 = 23, 37 – 15 = 22, 82 – 1 = 11, 95 – 51 = 44, 74 – 52 = 22, 67 – 55 = 12

Page 45: From start to finish: 314, 221, 272, 211, 37, 431, 231, 441, 522

Page 46: 1. yellow; **.** yellow; **3.** yellow; **.** green; **5.** green; **.** green; **7.** yellow; **.** green; **9.** green; **0.** green; **11.** yellow; **2.** green; **13.** green; **4.** green; **15.** yellow; **6.** yellow

Page 47: Answers will vary.

Page 48: 1. potato; **.** whale; **3.** road; **.** snowman; **5.** shoes; **.** rock; **7.** mirror; **.** lemon; **9.** rocket; **0.** song; **11.** maple; **2.** sled; **Extra:** Answers will vary.

Page 49: Answers will vary.

Page 50: 1. 1, 2; **2.** 1, 6; **.** 1, 4; **4.** 1, 0; **5.** 61, 92, 1, 91; **6.** 83, 83, 81, 83

Page 51: 1. 86, 70, 81, 63, 36, 42; **2.** 62, 41, 60, 92, 33, 80; **3.** 96, 94, 93, 33, 85, 51; **4.** 40, 84, 74, 48, 81, 71

Page 52: 1. 374, 716, 535, 492, 990, 762; **2.** 839, 685, 454, 365, 953, 715; **3.** 430, 902, 566, 591, 836, 448; **4.** 694, 265, 871, 683, 639, 218

Page 53: From left to right and top to bottom: 674, 923, 960, 575, 492, 363, 888, 580, 767, 590, 644, 796; riddle: MARBLE CAKE

Page 54: 1. lazy; **2.** mean; **3.** selfish; **4.** kind; **5.** helpful; **6.** strong

Page 55: 1. scared; **2.** worried; **3.** proud; **4.** disappointed

Page 57: 1. 8, 2, 1, 3, 7, 4, 5, 6; **2.** sighed, laughed, screamed, shouted, squealed, bellowed, snickered; **3.** 6; **4.** 350°F; **5.** 10–12 minutes; **6.** 2 dozen

Page 58: 1. 19, 19, 17, 29, 57; **2.** 59, 46, 38, 12, 17; **3.** 29, 9, 8, 19, 15; **4.** 28, 17, 37, 39, 18

Page 59: 1. 46, 36, 58, 7; **2.** 11, 19, 28, 77; **3.** 14, 48, 16, 69

Page 60: 1. 489, 149, 290, 199, 297, 107; **2.** 187, 842, 175, 182, 519, 109; **3.** 394, 308, 398, 209, 575, 232; **4.** 278, 802, 625, 491, 408, 734

Page 61: From left to right and top to bottom: 338, 739, 369, 267, 768, 395, 643, 484, 558, 611, 189, 165; riddle: THE PLYMOUTH ROCK

Page 62: 1. read books; **2.** same haircut and wear the same clothes; **3.** their pets; **4.** Rebecca lets her bird out of its cage. Neela keeps her mouse in its cage.

Page 64: Alligators: have rounded snouts, prefer fresh water, have wider upper jaws than lower jaws; Both: warm up in the sun, cool off in the water, eat fish, live in the water, can move fast, are fierce; Crocodiles: show many teeth when jaws are closed, have pointed snouts.

Page 65: 4, 1, 3, 6, 2, 5

Page 66: 1. 3:00; **2.** 2:30; **3.** 7:30; **4.** 12:30; **5.** 11:00; **6.** 6:00

Page 67:

1.
2.
3.
4.
5.
6.
7.
8.

Page 68: 1. 3:00, 7:15, 12:45, 2:25; **2.** 8:10, 10:30, 6:30, 5:20

Page 69: 1. 1:40, 40, 1; **2.** 4:35, 35, 4; **3.** 9:05, 5, 9; **4.** 12:45, 45, 12; **5.** 6:55, 55, 6; **6.** 2:30, 30, 2

Page 70: 1. B.; **2.** E.; **3.** D.; **4.** A.; **5.** C.; **6.** Answers will vary.

Page 73: 1. C.; **2.** B.; **3.** D.; **4.** A.

Page 74: 1. 25, 10, 10, 5, 50¢; **2.** 25, 5, 5, 35¢; **3.** 10, 10, 10, 5, 35¢; **4.** 25, 25, 1, 1, 52¢; **5.** 25, 5, 10, 40¢; **6.** 50, 10, 10, 70¢; **7.** 50, 50, 100¢ or $1.00; **8.** 50, 10, 5, 65¢

Page 75: 1. truck; **2.** ring; **3.** ball; **4.** balloon; **5.** necklace; **6.** drum

Page 77: Answers are approximate. Iggy's Inches: 4, 5, 3, 13; Slinky's Centimeters: 4, 11, 9, 3, 27

Page 81: 1. 3, 1, 5, 2, 4; **2.** C.; **3.** B.; **4.** D.; **5.** Answers will vary.

Page 82: 1. 1; **2.** 1; **3.** 1; **4.** 3; **5.** 2; **6.** 1

Page 83: 1. $\frac{1}{2}$; **2.** $\frac{1}{4}$; **3.** $\frac{2}{4}$; **4.** $\frac{3}{4}$; **5.** $\frac{1}{3}$; **6.** $\frac{2}{3}$

Page 84:

1.
2.
3.   4.
5.

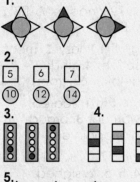

Page 85: 1. circle; **2.** square; **3.** circle; **4.** square; **5.** star; **6.** star

Page 87: 1. A.; **2.** C.; **3.** B.; **4.** A. Go back 1 space.; B. Go back 3 spaces.; C. Go back 2 spaces.; **5.** Hop to It!; **6.** 5 or older; **7.** No; **8.** trip; **9.** run; **10.** get; **11.** tire; **12.** cross

Page 88:

Page 89: 1. Yellow Sand; **2.** Evergreen Forest; **3.** yellow, sands; orange, desert; red, river; purple, mountains; **4.** play; **5.** dig; **6.** bury; **7.** miss; **8.** hunt; **9.** sky; **10.** tree; **11.** left; **12.** desert; **13.** lea **14.** Answers will vary.

Page 90: 1. 8; **2.** 8; **3.** 12 **4.** 12; Each problem should have the same number of marbles per bag.

Page 91: 1. 3 x 3; **2.** 3 x 3; **3.** 4 x 2; **4.** 5 x 1; **5.** 3 x 4; **6.** 3 x 1; **7.** 5 x 2; **8.** 4   1

Page 92: 1. 14 + 6 + 16 = 36 wild cats; **2.** 22 + 27 = 49 children; **3.** 16 3 = 19 parents; **4.** 132 + 68 = 200 tickets; **5.** 2 + 2 + 1 5 shows; **6.** 14 + 24 + 31 = 69 props

Page 93: 1. $3.00 – $2.38 = $0.62; **2.** $1.38 – $1.29 = $0.09; **3.** 26 – 14 = 12 cupcakes; **4.** 10 – = 7 sodas; **5.** $2.38 – $1.29 = $1.09; **6.** $1.50 – $1.29 = $0.21